Englisch
für kaufmännische Berufe
Grundkurs

von
Petra Lembke-Fuchs
Diane Redshaw
Barbara Ware-Thürwächter

Ernst Klett Verlag
Stuttgart Düsseldorf Leipzig

Englisch für kaufmännische Berufe

Grundkurs

von
Petra Lembke-Fuchs
Diane Redshaw
Barbara Ware-Thürwächter

Beratung:
Ulrich Engelbertz

Wörterverzeichnis:
Peter Bereza, Axel Ruland

Illustrationen:
Peter Byatt

9 783128 082004

1. Auflage A 1 11 10 9 8 | 2007 2006 2005

Alle Drucke dieser Auflage können im Unterricht nebeneinander benutzt werden. Die letzte Zahl bezeichnet das Jahr dieses Druckes.

Internetadresse: http:// www.klett-verlag.de

Redaktion: Margit Künzel, Volker Wendland
Einbandgestaltung: Elmar Feuerbach

Druck: Sfera International, Mailand. Printed in Italy.
ISBN 3-12-808200-6

Introduction

Vorwort

In einer Zeit zunehmender internationaler wirtschaftlicher Verflechtungen gehört die Beherrschung einer Fremdsprache heute in allen Bereichen des beruflichen und privaten Lebens zur allgemeinen Grundqualifikation.
Hierbei spielt Englisch als internationale Handels- und Verkehrssprache eine besonders wichtige Rolle.
Entsprechend den derzeitigen Lehrplänen für die kaufmännischen Berufsschulen der verschiedenen Bundesländer ist dieses Lehrwerk stark berufs- und anwendungsbezogen ausgerichtet. Besonderer Wert wird darauf gelegt, die englische Sprache als Mittel der Verständigung situationsgerecht und sprachlich angemessen einzusetzen.

Der Lernstoff gliedert sich in acht *Units*. Jede *Unit* ist in *Topics* (A, B, C usw.) unterteilt, die alle stark lerneraktiv aufgebaut sind und besonders diejenigen Fertigkeiten fördern, die im kaufmännisch-beruflichen Umfeld von Bedeutung sind (z.B. Kommunikation am Arbeitsplatz, am Telefon, auf Messen, Bearbeiten von Geschäftsbriefen, Umgang mit (ausländischen) Geschäftspartnern, Vorbereitungen von Geschäftsreisen, Vorbereitungen auf Vorstellungsgespräche usw.). Zahlreiche lernerzentrierte Aufgaben bieten die Möglichkeit, von Anfang an die Sprechfertigkeit zu schulen und den berufsbezogenen Wortschatz vor dem Hintergrund realistischer Geschäftsbeziehungen systematisch zu vertiefen und zu erweitern. Zum schnellen Nachschlagen von nützlichen Redemitteln dient eine jeweils zweisprachig angelegte Zusammenstellung von *Useful phrases* am Ende einer jeden Unit.

Neben dem Sprechen liegt ein weiterer wichtiger Schwerpunkt auf der Schulung des Hörverstehens. Dabei wird auch die Situation berücksichtigt, dass die miteinander kommunizierenden Geschäftspartner häufig keine englischsprachigen Muttersprachler sind. Auf der Kassette finden sich Texte und Dialoge aus den *Units* 1 bis 8. Das Symbol kennzeichnet jeweils die Teile, zu denen Tonaufnahmen vorliegen. Die Hörverständnistexte sind im Anhang des Lehrwerks abgedruckt.

Außerdem gibt es im Anhang eine Grammatik mit englisch-deutschen Beispielsätzen und verständlichen Regelerklärungen auf Deutsch sowie ein unitbegleitendes Wörterverzeichnis und ein alphabetisches Wortregister.

Viel Spaß und Erfolg beim Englischlernen mit *Englisch für kaufmännische Berufe!*

Ihr Grundkurs-Team

Contents
Inhalt

Quellennachweis

Cartoons

© Punch: 13, 22, 79, 116; Noel Watson, The Sunday Times (8 April 1990), © Times Newspapers Limited, 1990: 16; HERMAN © Jim Unger. Reprinted with permission of Universal Press Syndicate. All rights reserved.: 62; © Daily Mail/Solo: 78

Fotos

Brenda Boulton, Minehead, Somerset: 7 (Patricia Newman); Deutsche Messe AG, Hannover: 90; Dr. Hans-Werner Thunig, Winterbach: 7, 32, 50, 54, 56, 57, 83, 86, 91, 98, 112, 115

Realien

By permission of AT& T Deutschland GmbH: 34; Titelfoto "Holiday on Ice". In: Offiziellem Monatsprogramm des Fremdenverkehrsamtes der Landeshauptstadt München: 65; © Falk-Verlag AG, Hamburg: 66; Adapted from "Travelling in London". Maps and information to help you get around by London Transport Tourism. (All prices mentioned were correct at time of going to print.): 67; Katrin Schickentanz, Stuttgart: 67 (Photocard); Klett Archiv: 67 (One Day Travelcard, Seven Days Travelcard); © London Regional Transport Registered User Number 95/2286: 68

Texte

What's on in Munich? In: Offiziellem Monatsprogramm des Fremdenverkehrsamtes der Landeshauptstadt München: 65; Adapted from "Travelling in London". Maps and information to help you get around by London Transport Tourism. (All prices mentioned were correct at time of going to print.): 66, 67

In einigen Fällen ist es uns trotz intensiver Bemühungen nicht gelungen, die Rechte-Inhaber zu ermitteln. Wir bitten diese, sich mit dem Verlag in Verbindung zu setzen.

Alle Namen von Personen und Firmen sind frei erfunden. Eventuelle Ähnlichkeiten sind zufällig und nicht beabsichtigt.

Englisch für kaufmännische Berufe
Grundkurs

Lehrwerksteile

Schülerbuch:	Klett-Nr. 808200
Kassette:	Klett-Nr. 808220
Lehrerhandbuch:	Klett-Nr. 808210

Unit 1

The first day at a new job

Topic A

Meeting the people in Tim's department

Microware Ltd is a London-based computer services company with an office in Munich. Tim Schneider, who recently completed his training as an "Industriekaufmann" in Düsseldorf, has just joined the company as a marketing assistant. Since most of the staff are British, the company language is English.

Frank Williams

The organization of the marketing department

Patricia Newman

Tim Schneider

Jenny Rose

Martha Beyer

Miriam Tellmann

Marketing Manager
Assistant
Secretary
Marketing Assistants (2)
Secretary

a Look at the people around Tim and guess "who is who".

I think ... is the manager.
... could be the ...
Frank Williams looks like ...

b **Listen to the cassette and answer the following questions.**

1. Who is in charge of the department?
2. Who does Ms Beyer work for?
3. Who is Miriam Tellmann?
4. Who does Jenny Rose work for?

c **Now check your answers to "who is who" and read the dialogue with your partner.**

Patricia Newman, the assistant to the marketing manager, shows Tim around on his first day and introduces him to his co-workers.

Patricia Newman: Good morning, Tim. Nice to see you again. How are you?
Tim Schneider: Oh, I'm fine. Thank you.
Patricia Newman: I would like to show you around the marketing department this morning and introduce you to your co-workers.
Tim Schneider: Yes, that would be nice.
Patricia Newman: Of course, we work closely with the sales and advertising departments. Each department has its own small area. I won't introduce you to anyone there today, though. It might be too much for the first day.
Tim Schneider: Okay, that's fine.
Patricia Newman: Mr Williams, the marketing manager, isn't in today. You can meet him tomorrow, perhaps.
Tim Schneider: Yes, all right.
Patricia Newman: May I introduce you to Ms Beyer, our secretary. Ms Beyer works for Mr Williams and myself.
Martha, this is Tim Schneider, the new marketing assistant.
Martha Beyer: Hello, Tim. How do you do?
Tim Schneider: How do you do?
Patricia Newman: Good morning, Jenny. I'd like you to meet Tim Schneider. He's the new marketing assistant. He'll be working with Miriam.
Jenny Rose: Hello, Tim. Nice to meet you.
Patricia Newman: We have two secretaries for the sales, advertising and marketing departments. Jenny is one of them and she works with Monika Kühl.
Tim Schneider: Nice to meet you too, Ms Rose.
Jenny Rose: Oh, please call me Jenny.
Tim Schneider: Okay, Jenny.
Patricia Newman: Is Miriam in her office? I thought she could help Tim get settled in this morning.
Jenny Rose: She's just gone to see Anne Miller for a moment. Tim, would you like a cup of coffee until Miriam gets back?
Tim Schneider: Yes, thanks. I'd love one.
Patricia Newman: Okay, great. Tim, Jenny can introduce you to Miriam. She's our other marketing assistant. She can help you with any

	questions. But don't hesitate to call me if I can help you with anything.
Tim Schneider:	Thank you and thank you for showing me around, Ms Newman.
Patricia Newman:	Oh, you're very welcome. Goodbye for now.
Tim Schneider:	Goodbye.

Organization Chart Microware

Assistant
Julian Cole

Managing Director
Bill Reece

Secretary
Astrid Wagner

Personnel Department

Company Training Manager
Ruth Jansen

Secretary
Sally Jenkins

Advertising Department

Advertising Manager
Jill Thompson

Assistant to the Advertising Manager
Andreas Stone

Secretaries
Jenny Rose
Monika Kühl

Advertising Assistants
Thomas Probst
Anne Miller

Research and Development Department

Research Manager
Tom Windsor

Finance Department

Chief Accountant
Marion Bauer

Secretary
Brenda Lewis

Sales Department

Sales Manager
Morris Brown

Assistant to the Sales Manager
Margit Anderson

Secretaries
Janet MacDonald
Brigit Becker

Sales Assistants
Marianne Baumgart
Georg Schmidt

Marketing Department

Marketing Manager
Frank Williams

Assistant to the Marketing Manager
Patricia Newman

Secretaries
Martha Beyer
Susan Davidson

Marketing Assistants
Tim Schneider
Miriam Tellmann

d Now draw an organization chart of the company where you work. Introduce it to the rest of the class.

Keep in mind

How do you do? (fälschlicherweise häufig im Sinne von *Wie geht es dir/Ihnen?* gebraucht) ist lediglich eine Begrüßungsfloskel, die mit *How do you do?* erwidert wird und nur bei der ersten Begegnung zusammen mit einem Händedruck verwendet wird.

How are you? ist eine Frage nach dem Befinden des Gegenübers und erwartet von daher auch eine Antwort im Sinne von *Fine, thanks, and you?* Ist die Antwort weniger erfreulich *Not too good, I'm afraid,* dann ist es üblich, sich nach der Ursache für das schlechte Befinden zu erkundigen, z.B. *What's the matter?*

Die Anrede mit Vornamen ist in amerikanischen und britischen Firmen gebräuchlicher als in deutschen Firmen.

Die Anrede mit *Ms* (für verheiratete und unverheiratete Frauen) anstelle von *Mrs* (nur für verheiratete Frauen) oder *Miss* (nur für ledige Frauen) setzt sich immer mehr durch.

Die abgekürzten Formen *Mr, Mrs* und *Ms* können mit oder ohne Punkt geschrieben werden. Im Amerikanischen steht hier jeweils ein Punkt.

e Match the phrases on the left with the replies on the right. Which of the phrases are to be used more likely in formal or informal language?

1. How do you do?	A. Thank you.
2. How are you?	B. Hi!
3. Nice to meet you.	C. Hello, Jenny. Nice to meet you.
4. I'd like you to meet ...	D. It's a pleasure to meet you.
5. Welcome to Microware Inc.	E. Hello, ... How do you do?
6. This is Jenny Rose.	F. Nice to meet you, too.
7. May I introduce you to Ms Beyer?	G. How do you do?
8. Have you met ...?	H. I'm fine, thank you.
9. How are you doing?	I. Fine, thanks. And you?
10. Hi!	J. No, I don't think we've met before.

f Role play.
Use the organization chart on page 9 to introduce Mr Jones formally and informally. The phrases in exercise e may help you.

Mr Jones, a visitor, is coming to Microware in Munich.

Examples:

Student A: Ms Beyer? May I introduce you to Mr Jones from Dataprint in New Zealand?

(Student B and C both shake hands)

Student B: How do you do, Mr Jones?
Student C: How do you do, Ms Beyer?

Student A: Good morning, Anne.
Student B: Morning, Janet. Have you met Bob Jones from Dataprint in New Zealand?
Student A: Hello, Bob. Nice to meet you. I'm Janet MacDonald.
Student C: Nice to meet you, too. Anne's told me that you two are ...

g Work in pairs. Complete some of the questions below and match them with a suitable answer. Then think of further possible questions and answers.

Over dinner Anne Miller wants to find out more about Mr Jones, the visitor from Dataprint. She asks him a lot of questions.

Example:

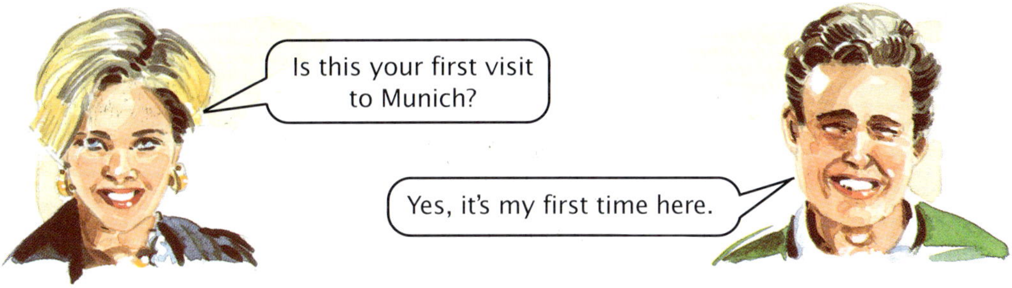

Student A:

1. Have you been to ... before?
2. What do you think of ...?
3. How do you find the people?
4. How do you like ...?
5. What do you do in your free time?
6. Have you got a ...?
7. How do you like the food?
8. ~~Is this your first visit to Munich?~~

Student B:

A. ~~Yes, it's my first time here.~~
B. I play tennis/golf/football.
C. I really enjoy it – it's very tasty.
D. Yes, I've got two children./No, I'm single/divorced/a confirmed bachelor.
E. Really nice, and very friendly.
F. Yes, I came three years ago.
G. I like fishing/jazz music/cycling/surfing.
H. (I think) it's wonderful.

Topic B

The office

a Match the following items (1–20) with the objects in the picture. Use the plural where necessary.

1. filing cabinet
2. shelf/shelves
3. printer
4. in-tray/out-tray
5. telephone
6. monitor
7. notice board
8. file
9. fax (machine)
10. wastepaper basket
11. stapler
12. hole punch
13. keyboard
14. calculator
15. photocopier
16. mouse
17. computer
18. (laser) printer
19. disk
20. answering machine

b Look at the picture again on page 12 and say where the items (1–20) are. Use the words in the box.

Example:
The telephone is **on** Tim's desk.

on	next to	behind	below
under	in front of	on top of	on the left/right
by	near	opposite	between

c Now describe your workplace in the same way. Use your dictionary if necessary.

d Read the dialogue with your partner.

Miriam shows Tim around the office.

Miriam: So, this is our office. I'm sure we'll get on well together. The office is big enough for two people.
Tim: Yes, it's quite big and very bright.
Miriam: This is my desk here and that's your desk with your telephone and computer over there.
Tim: Oh yes, that's fine.
Miriam: These shelves are for current surveys and those over there are for completed surveys.
Tim: What are these filing cabinets for? I thought most information was on disks these days.
Miriam: Yes, you're right. But these files date back quite a few years. We are working on putting the old files onto disks but it's a lot of work.
Tim: Yes, I can imagine that.
Miriam: These are your in- and out-trays. This is the photocopier and over there is the fax machine. They are both very easy to operate.
By the way, do you drink tea or coffee?
Tim: I usually drink coffee.
Miriam: Oh, that's good. The coffee machine is over there in the corner. Coffee, sugar and powdered milk are in the cupboard above it.
Tim: Right.
Miriam: Do you have any questions?
Tim: Well ...

"Goodnight, Miss Travis, I've finished my coffee, but I've left my biscuit. Put it in my in-tray and I'll deal with it tomorrow."

e Decide if the following statements are true or false. If they are false, correct them.

1. Miriam and Tim are going to work in different offices.
2. Tim likes the office.
3. Tim doesn't have his own telephone and computer.
4. The shelves are for current and completed surveys.
5. The files in the filing cabinet are from last year.
6. Copying files onto disks is a lot of work.
7. Miriam and Tim use the same in- and out-trays.
8. The fax machine is easy to operate; the photocopier is difficult to operate.
9. Tim has to take a course to learn how to operate the machines in the office.
10. Tim prefers coffee to tea.

f Think of some questions Tim might want to ask Miriam.

Examples:

Where can I order typing paper?

What is the extension number of the advertising department?

What is Ms Beyer's extension?

Topic C

Office duties

a Work in pairs. One person asks for certain things to be done and the other gives a suitable reply.

Example:

Could you go down to the reception to get the keys?

Sure. Right now?

Student A: Make requests with *could* and *would*. Use the information in the box.

1. make an appointment with Ms Müller
2. type this letter (It's rather urgent.)
3. meet Mr Rogers at the airport for me
4. send a fax to Mr Jones in New Zealand
5. pick up the parcel in the post room
6. make some more coffee

Student B: Answer your partner's requests with a suitable response. The following phrases will help you.

A. No problem. What time is he ...?
B. Sure.
C. Certainly, .../Of course.
D. Certainly, but I've got to finish ... first.
E. I've already sent/asked ...
F. I'm rather busy right now. Can ...?

b Now think of more things to ask your partner to do. He or she will give you a suitable reply.

c Work in pairs. One person offers to do certain things and the other gives a suitable reply.

Example:

Would you like me to book a table for you?

Oh, that would be really helpful.

Student A: Make offers with *would*. Draw your own "word lobster" and fill the "legs" with examples of your own.

Would you like
- *me to take you to the airport?*
- ______
- *Ms Beyer to call you a taxi?*
- ______
- *Jenny to write the reports for you?*

Student B: Answer your partner's questions with a suitable reply. The following phrases may help you.

> That's very kind of you.
>
> Thank you, I'd like it very much.
>
> Yes please, if it's no trouble/bother.
>
> Yes please, if you don't mind.
>
> That would be wonderful.

d Match the words (1–10) with the words (A–J).

Example:
1. meet – E. a visitor

1. ~~meet~~	A. a company
2. do	B. a report
3. make	C. a meeting
4. write	D. late
5. send	E. ~~a visitor~~
6. visit	F. a business trip
7. distribute	G. the filing
8. go on	H. a fax
9. work	I. a photocopy
10. go to	J. the mail

e How often do you do the things in exercise d? Use the words in the box.

Example:
I **occasionally** meet a visitor at the airport.

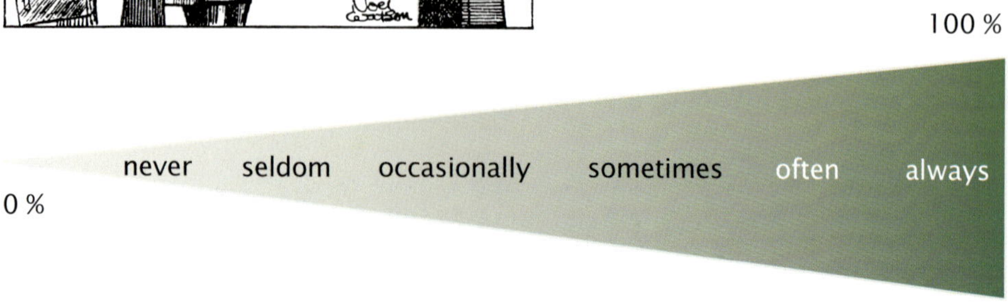

Topic D

Giving directions

1. Turn right. ↱ Turn left. ↰ Go straight ahead. ↑

2.

Go up to the second floor.

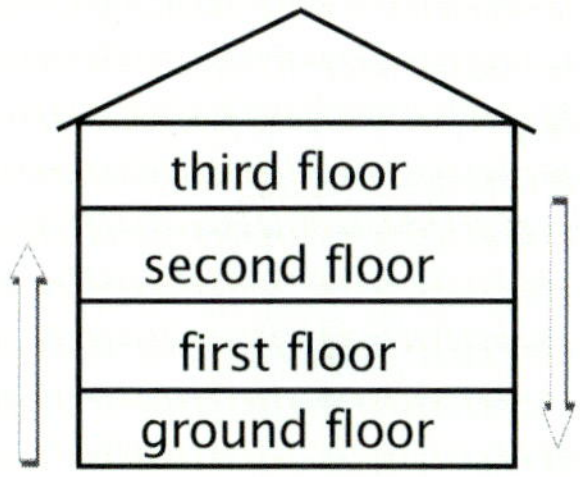

Go down to the ground floor.

3. Go down the stairs.

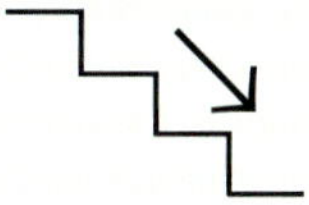

Go up the stairs.

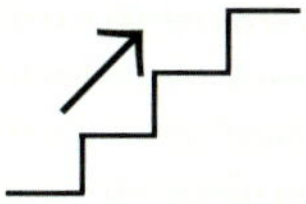

4. Go down the corridor.
Go along the corridor.

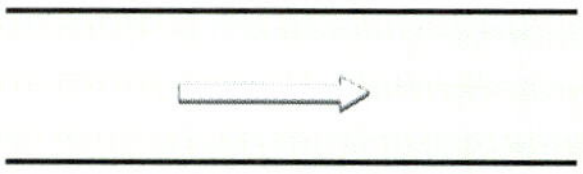

5. Go across the lounge.

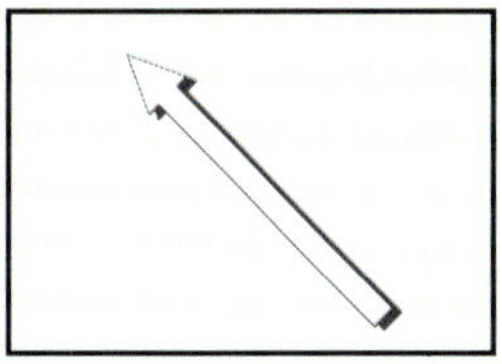

6. The canteen is on the right-hand side.
The canteen is on your right.

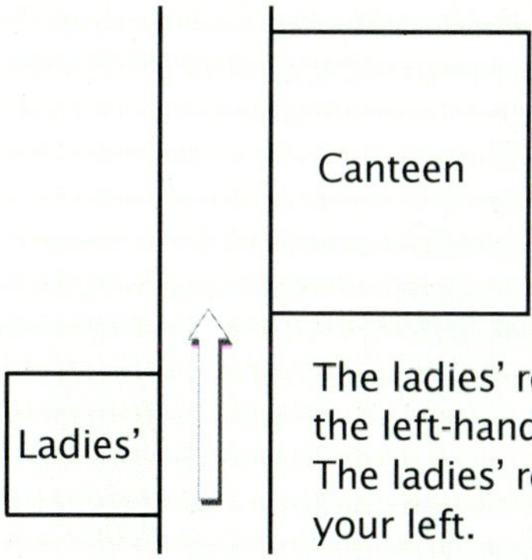

The ladies' room is on the left-hand side.
The ladies' room is on your left.

Keep in mind

Die Stockwerk- bzw. Etagenbezeichnung eines Hauses unterscheidet sich in Großbritannien und in den USA.

Großbritannien: *ground floor* (Erdgeschoss), *first floor* (1. Stockwerk) usw.

USA: *first floor* (Erdgeschoss), *second floor* (1. Stockwerk) usw.

lift (BE)/elevator (AE)

Office Building Layout

Ground floor **Finance and Personnel Department**

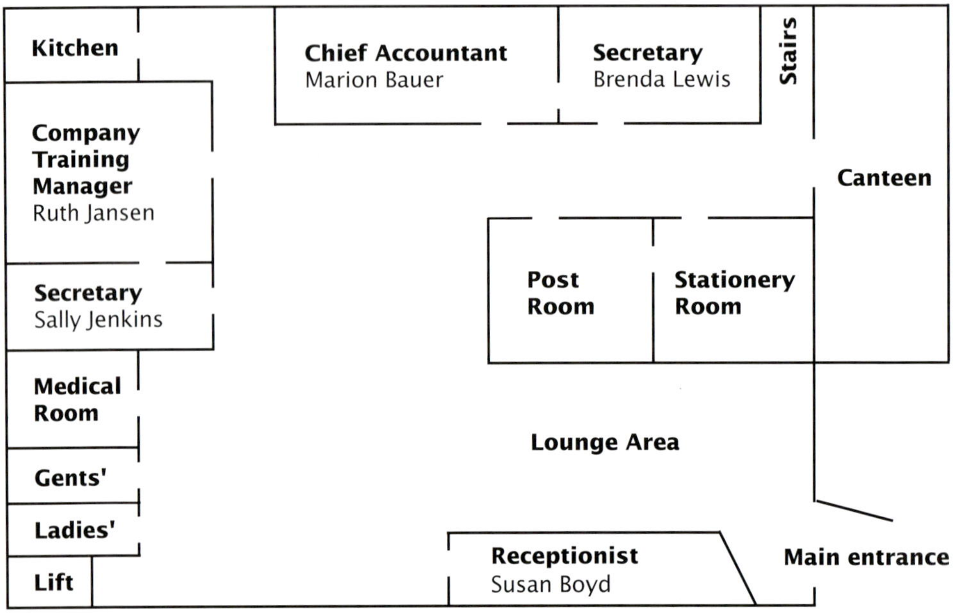

First floor **Marketing and Sales Department**

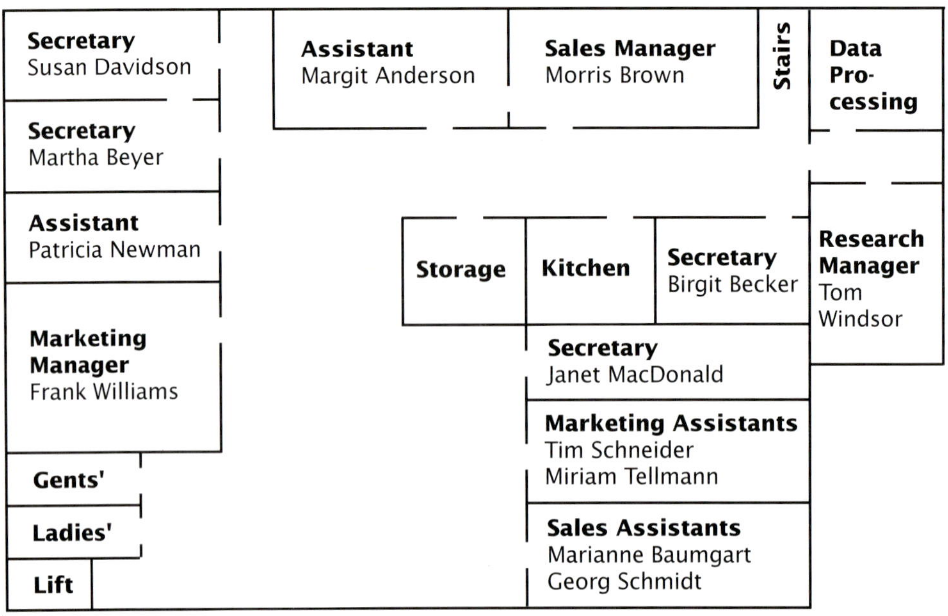

Second floor **Advertising Department**

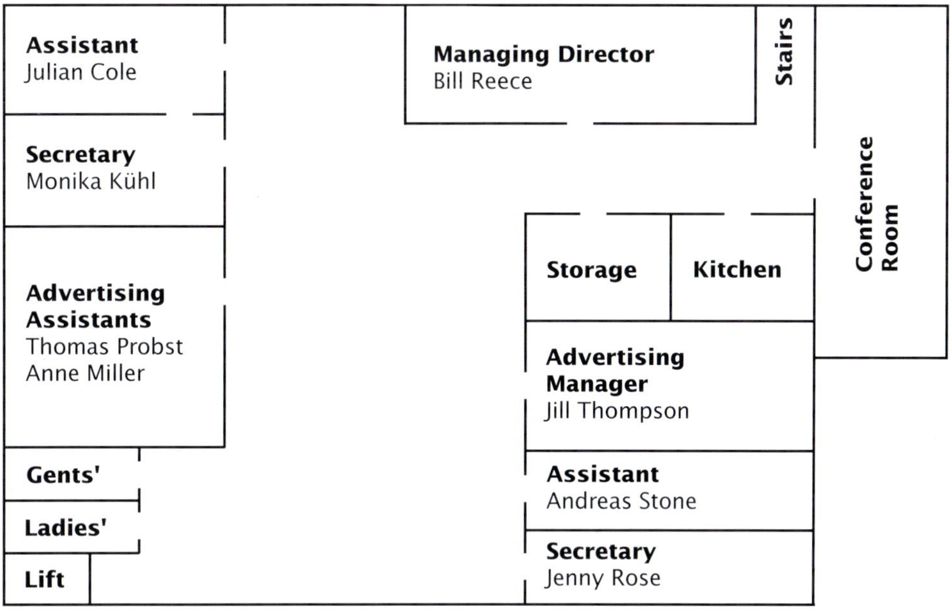

a **Listen to the cassette and follow Tim on his way through the office building. Where does he go?**

1. Tim is at the main entrance.
2. Tim is in Andreas Stone's office.
3. Tim is in his office.

b **Work in pairs. Explain to your partner where certain rooms are in the building. Use the chart on pages 18 and 19.**

1. Your partner is at the reception desk.
   Could you tell me the way to Ms Newman's office, please?
2. Your partner is in Ms Newman's office.
   Could you tell me the way to the canteen, please?
3. Your partner is in Tim's office.
   Where is the data processing room, please?
4. Your partner is in Janet MacDonald's office.
   I have to go to the medical room. Would you mind telling me how to get there?

c Work in groups. Ask for directions in the building. Use the chart on pages 18 and 19.

Examples:
You are in the canteen. You want to go to the conference room.
You are in the post room. You ask for the way to ...

Useful phrases

1. Introducing oneself and other people

Formal:

How do you do? I'm .../My name's ...	Guten Tag. Ich bin .../Ich heiße ...
May I introduce you to ... ?/I'd like you to meet ...	Darf ich Ihnen ... vorstellen?/Ich möchte Ihnen ... vorstellen.
Pleased to meet you.	Es freut mich, Sie kennen zu lernen.

Informal:

Hello, my name's ...	Hallo, ich bin .../ich heiße ...
How are you? (How are you doing?)	Wie geht's?
Fine, thanks. And you?	Danke, gut. Und dir/Ihnen?
Klaus, this is John.	Klaus, das ist John.
Nice to meet you.	Schön, dich kennen zu lernen.

2. Asking the way and giving directions

Could you tell me the way to ...?	Könnten Sie mir den Weg nach/zu ... sagen?
I'm looking for ...	Ich suche ...
Where is ...?	Wo ist ...?
Is there a ... nearby?	Gibt es ... in der Nähe?
Excuse me, I'm looking for the ...	Entschuldigung, ich suche ...
Go straight ahead ...	Gehen Sie geradeaus ...
Turn left/right.	Biegen Sie links/rechts ab.
Take the first/second on your left/right.	Nehmen Sie die erste/zweite Straße links/rechts.
Go up/down to the first/second floor.	Gehen Sie zur ersten/zweiten Etage hinauf/hinunter.
Take the lift (elevator) to ...	Nehmen Sie den Aufzug zur/zum ...
Go across the lounge ...	Gehen Sie quer durch den Salon ...
It is on the right/left-hand side.	Es ist auf der rechten/linken Seite.
The ... is opposite/next to ...	Der/Die/Das ... ist gegenüber/neben ...

Unit 2

Telephoning

Topic A

How to make a telephone call

**a Which of these points do you find most important when you have to make or receive a phone call in English?
Compare your answers with your partner.**

1. trying to speak clearly
2. sounding polite and agreeable
3. speaking slowly
4. making sure your call is brief
5. have all necessary information at hand
6. saying who you want to speak to
7. confirming that you have understood everything
8. saying where you are calling from
9. saying precisely who you are
10. have pen and paper ready

b Complete the sentences with the words from the box.

1. You look up the number in the ①.
2. You pick up the ②.
3. You dial the number for a ③.
4. If you want to make a ④ you dial first the ⑤, then the ⑥ and finally the number.
5. If the line is ⑦ or if it is ⑧, try again.

> international code
> very bad
> long-distance call
> telephone directory
> local call
> receiver
> area code
> engaged (BE), busy (AE)

c Match the countries with the capitals.

1. Canada	9. Holland/The Netherlands	A. Wellington	H. Canberra
2. U.S.A.	10. Poland	B. Ottawa	I. Athens
3. Australia	11. Spain	C. Edinburgh	J. Brussels
4. New Zealand	12. Belgium	D. Stockholm	K. Lisbon
5. Wales	13. Greece	E. Oslo	L. Amsterdam
6. Scotland	14. Hungary	F. Cardiff	M. Budapest
7. Norway	15. Portugal	G. Washington D.C.	N. Warsaw
8. Sweden			O. Madrid

d Look at exercise c again. What do you call someone who comes from each of these countries? Use your dictionary if necessary.

Example:
Canada – Canadian

"Do say if there's anyone you don't know."

Keep in mind

Nationalitätsbezeichnungen sowie Personen- und Sprachbezeichnungen werden im Englischen immer großgeschrieben.

Topic B

Requesting information on the telephone

a **Listen to the cassette.**

Susan Boyd: Microware. Guten Morgen.
Mr Lopez: Good morning, this is Mr Lopez from Electro Sul, Brazil. I'd like to talk to Mr Schneider.
Susan Boyd: Just a moment, Sir. I'll put you through. What was the name, please?
Mr Lopez: Lopez, Carlos Lopez.
Susan Boyd: Could you spell that, please?
Mr Lopez: Yes, that's L.O.P.E.Z.
Susan Boyd: Thank you. Hold the line, please.
Oh, I'm sorry, Mr Lopez, but Mr Schneider is not in his office. Would you like to leave a message?
Mr Lopez: Yes, could you please tell him that I called and that I'll try again this afternoon.
Susan Boyd: Certainly, and you can dial directly. His extension number is 803.
Mr Lopez: Thank you, goodbye.

b **Answer these questions on the dialogue.**

1. Who is calling?
2. Where is the caller from?
3. Who does the caller want to talk to?
4. What does the person called ask the caller to do?
5. What is Mr Schneider's extension number?

c **Listen to the cassette again. Then write down as many phrases as you can remember used by the caller and the person called.**

Example:

Caller	Person called
... this is Mr Lopez ...	Just a moment, Sir.
I'd like to talk to ...	I'll put you through.

d **Complete the conversation with appropriate phrases.**

Receptionist: Maxwell & Sons. Good afternoon.
You: ① *(Mr Sander)*
Receptionist: Hold the line, please. I'll put you through.

You: ②
Receptionist: I'm sorry, Mr Sander's not in his office.
You: ③
Receptionist: No, I'm afraid I don't know when he'll be back. Would you like to leave a message?
You: ④
Receptionist: All right. You can dial directly. His extension number is 874.
You: ⑤
Receptionist: You're welcome. Goodbye.

e **Listen to the cassette and fill in the missing information.**

call	**1**	**2**	**3**	**4**
caller's name	Robert	?	?	?
person or company called	?	?	?	?
call is from	?	?	Paris	?
phone number (person called)	?	/	/	?

f **Match the sentences on the left with a suitable response on the right.**

1. When would be the best time to reach her?
2. Could you connect me with Ms Winter, please?
3. Is that 890 166?
4. Thank you very much, good-bye.
5. Is Mr Jones in?
6. Frank Raleigh.
7. What about Monday?
8. I'm afraid I can't come to the meeting on Friday.

A. Sorry, I think you've got the wrong number.
B. You're welcome, goodbye.
C. I'm afraid he's not in the office today.
D. Oh, I'm afraid I can't. I'm going to Brussels on Monday.
E. Could we fix another date?
F. She'll be here in the afternoon.
G. Hold the line, please. I'll put you through.
H. Could you repeat your surname, please?

g **Role play. Sit back to back with a partner and make an imaginary phone call. The following situation may help you.**

Student A: Phone Comptex company and ask for Ms Candy.
Student B: Try to connect Student A and tell him or her that Ms Candy is not in her office.
Student A: Leave a message and make an appointment for Tuesday instead of Wednesday.
Student B: Say that you will give Ms Candy the message.

Keep in mind

Bei Telefonnummern werden im Englischen die Ziffern einzeln gesprochen. Sie können dabei in rhythmische Zweier-, Dreier- oder auch Vierergruppen aufgeteilt werden. Wenn in einer solchen Gruppe zwei Ziffern gleich sind, z.B. 66, werden sie meist *double six* ausgesprochen. Im Amerikanischen ist *double six* nicht üblich.

406604 *four oh/double six/oh four* oder *four oh six/six oh four.*
oh /əʊ/ (BE) oder *zero* (AE)

In Großbritannien ist es üblich, sich am Telefon privat entweder mit der eigenen Telefonnummer oder mit *Hello* zu melden. In Amerika ist es unüblich, sich mit der Telefonnummer zu melden; *hello* ist hier gebräuchlich.

Absagen am Telefon sollten im Englischen mit einem höflichen Ausdruck des Bedauerns eingeleitet werden (z.B. *I'm sorry/I'm afraid* ...).

Topic C

Making arrangements

a **Work in pairs. Read the dialogue and complete the missing parts with the words from the box. Then listen to the cassette and check your answers.**

See you	What about	participate in that fair
manage	meet you	get in touch

Tim Schneider: Schneider speaking.
Carlos Lopez: Hello, Mr Schneider. This is Carlos Lopez from Electro Sul, Brazil. Mr Williams told me to (1) with you. He said you could help us with the organization for our stand at the fair in Boston. You know this will be the first time that we are going to (2) .
Tim Schneider: That's right, Mr Williams informed me about that.
Carlos Lopez: I'm in Munich right now and I would like to (3) and discuss some of the details.
Tim Schneider: That's a good idea. Well, let me see. (4) tomorrow morning? Could you (5) to come to my office at 10 o'clock?
Carlos Lopez: Yes, that's fine. I'll be there. (6) then. Goodbye.
Tim Schneider: Goodbye.

b Look at the pictures and match the verbs with the nouns.

1. have	A. a fair
2. play	B. a staff meeting
3. meet	C. breakfast
4. attend	D. a business partner
5. discuss	E. tennis
6. visit	F. reports

a

b

c

d

e

f

c Look at Tim's time planner with arrangements for next week. Match his arrangements with a time from the box and make up sentences as in the example.

Example:
Tim's meeting Mr Lopez, a business partner, on Monday morning.

Friday afternoon	Thursday morning
~~Monday morning~~	Tuesday afternoon
Wednesday evening	Sunday morning
Saturday evening	

Mon	14	~~*10am meet Mr Lopez (a business partner)*~~
Tues	15	*2pm discuss reports on market research (Ms Newman)*
Wed	16	*visit fair in Frankfurt* *7pm go to reception (Sic Hotel)*
Thurs	17	*9.30am breakfast (Mr Coleman)*
Fri	18	*2.30pm attend staff meeting*
Sat	19	*7pm Mum's birthday party*
Sun	**20**	*11am tennis (Susan)*

Keep in mind

Gewöhnlich wird im Englischen für 14.00 oder 15.00 Uhr *2pm* oder *3pm* gesagt. Im Reiseverkehr gilt die 24-Stunden-Zählung.

am: Abkürzung für *ante meridiem* (lat. vor der Mitte des Tages): von Mitternacht bis Mittag

pm: Abkürzung für *post meridiem* (lat. nach der Mitte des Tages): von Mittag bis Mitternacht

12.00 *am:* gesprochen *noon*/12.00 *pm:* gesprochen *midnight*

d Work in pairs. Write down your arrangements for next week. Then phone your partner to arrange a meeting. Use the flowchart as a guide.

I'd like to arrange a meeting.
Are you free on ... afternoon?
Does ... afternoon suit you?

↘

I'm sorry I'm afraid	I'm ... ing. I have to ...	in the afternoon.

↙

What How	about tomorrow afternoon?

↘

Yes, that's fine.
Is *(time)* okay?

↙

Yes, that's perfect. See you tomorrow afternoon at *(time)*.

e Role play. Read the information below and prepare the role play with your partner(s). Make notes if necessary. Act out the role play in class.

1. *(2 roles)* Call Ms Winter and arrange a meeting on Monday 3rd.(*month*). Ms Winter is busy that day. Try to find another date.
2. *(2 roles)* Mr Duclos is a customer of yours. He is spending several days in your town. Call at the hotel where he is staying and ask for him. Invite him for dinner the same evening.
3. *(3 roles)* You are planning a business trip to New York for next month. Call Printex Inc. New York and ask to speak to Janet Hudson. The secretary will tell you that Ms Hudson is not in the office. Leave a message for her to call you back. Give your telephone number and the time you will be in the office. When Ms Hudson calls back you both check your diary and arrange a meeting in New York.

Topic D

Numbers and names

a **Work in pairs. Dictate the telephone numbers (1–5) to your partner. Your partner will then dictate the numbers (6–10) to you.**

Example:
420 223
four two oh double two three or *four two zero two two three*

1. 001 818 723 9434
2. 0055 21 965 3714
3. 0039 6427 3033
4. 0081 3667 7092
5. 0059 660 9440
6. 733 5688
7. 3388 569 7711
8. 518 9354
9. 112 544 688 7557
10. 833 449

b **Spell the names of these companies. Look at the English alphabet if necessary.**

OORA SKY Fujtsu PRODAC rh AB

a	b	c	d	e	f	g	h	i	j	k	l	m	n
[eɪ]	[biː]	[siː]	[diː]	[iː]	[ef]	[dʒiː]	[eɪtʃ]	[aɪ]	[dʒeɪ]	[keɪ]	[el]	[em]	[en]
o	p	q	r	s	t	u	v	w		x	y	z	
[əʊ]	[piː]	[kjuː]	[aː(r)]	[es]	[tiː]	[juː]	[viː]	['dʌbljuː]		[eks]	[waɪ]	[zed]*BE*, [ziː]*AE*	

c **Work in pairs. In turns spell these names. Look at the English alphabet if necessary.**

1. Spiekermann
2. Möller
3. Czernik
4. Yüksel
5. Weizenkorn
6. Hagel
7. Schmitt
8. Johnson
9. Meyer
10. Turm
11. Hill
12. Gunert
13. Rebell
14. Zarendorf
15. Krysanth

Keep in mind

Umlaute, wie z.B. ö oder ü werden im Englischen gewöhnlich als /əʊ/ /iː/, /juː/ /iː/ buchstabiert.

d Match the punctuation marks (1–10) with the expressions (A–J).

1.	.	A.	(double) quotation marks, inverted commas
2.	-	B.	exclamation mark
3.	!	C.	dash
4.	“ ”	D.	full stop (BE), period (AE)
5.	( )	E.	hyphen
6.	[ ]	F.	colon
7.	?	G.	stroke (BE), slash (AE)
8.	–	H.	(round) brackets, parentheses
9.	/	I.	question mark
10.	:	J.	(square) brackets

e Work in pairs.

Student A: Give your partner the following information over the phone. Be as precise as possible.

Student B: Write down exactly what your partner dictates to you. Then compare your notes with your partner's.

1. ... his name is Schulze-Wagenbach. That's S.C.H.U. ...
2. ... the meeting is on 1st September 1995, 10.35.
3. ... opening hours are Monday to Friday from 9 am – 6.30 pm.
4. ... the order no. is 03/415 B
5. ... BA flight no. 577 delayed.

f Listen to the cassette. Write down the two phone messages that are given.

PHONE MESSAGE

FOR: *Tim Schneider*

DATE: *30 May*

FROM: *Mr Lopez*

PHONE: *005511-829-6077*

☐ Will call again
☒ Please call
☐ Wants to see you

Message: *Please call Mr Lopez today before 5 pm or any time tomorrow.*

Message taken by: *Jenny Rose*

Topic E

Making reservations

a **Work in pairs. Read the dialogue with your partner and complete Tim's part. Then listen to the cassette and check your answer.**

Receptionist:	TFC Boston, can I help you?
Tim Schneider:	Hello, this is Tim Schneider calling from Microware in Munich. I'd like to make a reservation for the PC World Fair this spring. Could you connect me with the person in charge, please?
Receptionist:	Yes, Sir. Hold on, please.
Mary O'Neill:	Hello, Mr Schneider. How are you? I bet you're calling to reserve a stand for the fair next spring.
Tim Schneider:	[...]
Mary O'Neill:	Let me see. Just a moment, Mr Schneider. I'll check to see if your stand is still available. Last year you had stand no. 332. Luckily it's still available. Stand no. 333 next to it is available as well.
Tim Schneider:	I'm glad to hear that. Could you confirm our reservation as soon as possible?
Mary O'Neill:	Certainly. I'll send you a fax this afternoon.
Tim Schneider:	Thank you very much for your help, Ms O'Neill. I look forward to seeing you at the fair.
Mary O'Neill:	Thank's for calling. Goodbye.

b **Listen to the cassette again. Decide if the following statements are true or false. If they are false, correct them.**

1. It is the first time that Microware participates in the fair in Boston.
2. Mary O'Neill asked Tim to spell the name Microware.
3. The fair takes place in autumn.
4. Mary O'Neill reserves two stands for Microware.
5. The stand for Electro Sul is the bigger one.
6. Mary O'Neill promises to confirm the reservation per fax.

c Work in pairs. Put the dialogue in the right order. Then read it out with your partner to the rest of the class.

Hello, Mr Schneider. How are you? — B

I'm glad to hear that. — A

Certainly. I'll send you a fax this afternoon. — B

Yes, we're going to participate again. — A

Let me see. I'll check if your stand is still available. — B

Goodbye. — B

We'd like to reserve the same stand we had last year. — A

Thanks for calling. — B

Hello, this is Tim Schneider calling. — A

Last year you had stand no. 332. Luckily it's still available. — B

Thank you very much for your help. — A

Could you confirm our reservation as soon as possible? — A

I look forward to seeing you at the fair. — A

I bet you're calling to reserve a stand for the fair next spring. — B

d Translate into English.

Tim Schneider ruft TFC Boston an und spricht mit Mary O'Neill.

Tim Schneider: Ich möchte eine Reservierung für die PC Weltmesse im Frühjahr machen. Könnte ich bitte den gleichen Stand wie im letzten Jahr reservieren?

Mary O'Neill: Einen Augenblick bitte, Herr Schneider. Ich schaue nach, ob Ihr Stand noch frei ist.
Sie haben Glück, Herr Schneider. Der Stand ist noch zu haben.

Tim Schneider: Könnten Sie mir bitte die Reservierung so bald wie möglich bestätigen?

Mary O'Neill: Selbstverständlich. Ich schicke Ihnen heute Nachmittag ein Fax.

e Read the advertisement and answer the following questions.
Use your dictionary if necessary.

1. What do you have to do if you want to apply for an AT&T Calling Card?
2. How much do they charge you for getting one?
3. What are the advantages of an AT&T Calling Card?

IT'S NOT JUST

These days, you can call on your AT&T Calling Card to do more things from more places

A CALLING CARD,

then ever before. Together with AT&T USADirect Service, the Calling Card lets you dial direct

IT'S A GREETING CARD,

or access an English-speaking operator who can complete your call to the U.S. or to

IT'S A SHOPPING CARD,

any of over 45 countries with new AT&T ***World Connect*** *Service. Use the Calling Card to keep*

IT'S A BUSINESS CARD,

up with your family and friends. To call and order clothes from your favorite store.

IT'S A FAX CARD,

Or to check in with your bank. You can fax with it, set up conference calls, even get

IT'S A CONFERENCE CARD,

translation service. All at AT&T economical international rates. And all itemized on

IT'S A TRANSLATION CARD,

one monthly bill. Apply for your Calling Card by phone. In Germany, call AT&T at 0130-838888.

IT'S A SAVINGS CARD,

We may call it a Calling Card, but you'll find you can call it a lot more.

AND GETTING ONE IS FREE.

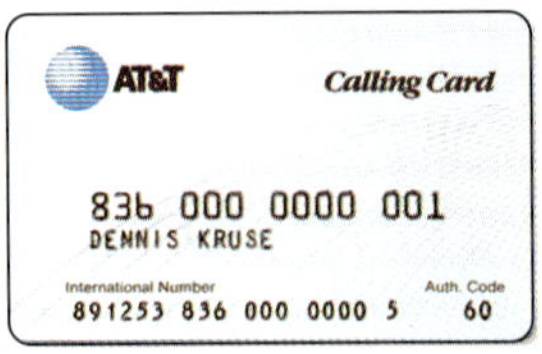

THE AT&T CALLING CARD.

Useful phrases

Telephoning

1. Opening

Person calling

Good morning./Hello. This is/It's ...	Guten Tag, hier ist/spricht ...
I'd like to speak to ...	Ich möchte gerne (mit) ... sprechen.
Could/Can I speak to ...	Könnte/kann ich (mit) ... sprechen?
Could you put me through to/ connect me with ...?	Könnten Sie mich bitte mit ... verbinden?
Extension 703, please.	Bitte die Durchwahl 703.
Is that 348 1991?	Spreche ich mit ... ?

Person called

Good morning./Hello.	Guten Tag.
Who's calling, please?	Wer ist am Apparat?
Hold on, please. I'll get him/her.	Warten Sie bitte. Ich hole ihn/sie.
I'm sorry he/she is not in.	Es tut mir Leid. Er/sie ist nicht da.
The line's busy. Will you hold?	Die Leitung ist besetzt. Bleiben Sie bitte am Apparat.
Would you mind calling back?	Würde es Ihnen etwas ausmachen, zurückzurufen?
Would you like to leave a message?	Möchten Sie gerne eine Nachricht hinterlassen?
Sorry (I think) you've got the wrong number.	Sie sind leider falsch verbunden.

2. Giving the message

Person calling

I'm phoning about ...	Ich rufe an wegen ...
Please tell him/her I called.	Sagen Sie ihm/ihr bitte, dass ich angerufen habe.
Could you take/give a message, please?	Könnten Sie bitte etwas ausrichten?

Person called

I'll give him/her a message.	Ich werde es ihm/ihr ausrichten.

3. Closing

Person calling

Thanks for your help.	Vielen Dank für Ihre/deine Hilfe.
I'll look forward to seeing/meeting you.	Ich freue mich darauf, Sie/dich zu sehen/treffen.
I'll phone again tomorrow.	Ich rufe morgen wieder an.
I'll try again later.	Ich versuche es später noch einmal.
Goodbye (then).	Auf Wiederhören.
Goodbye for now.	(Jetzt) erst einmal auf Wiederhören.

Person called

You're welcome.	Gern geschehen.
That's all right.	Keine Ursache
Thank you for calling.	Vielen Dank für Ihren/deinen Anruf.
Goodbye. *(formal)*	Auf Wiederhören.
Bye. *(informal)*	Wiederhören.

UNIT 3

Commercial correspondence

Topic A

Writing a business letter

Tim has to answer letters concerning products his company presented at the London Commu-2000 Fair.

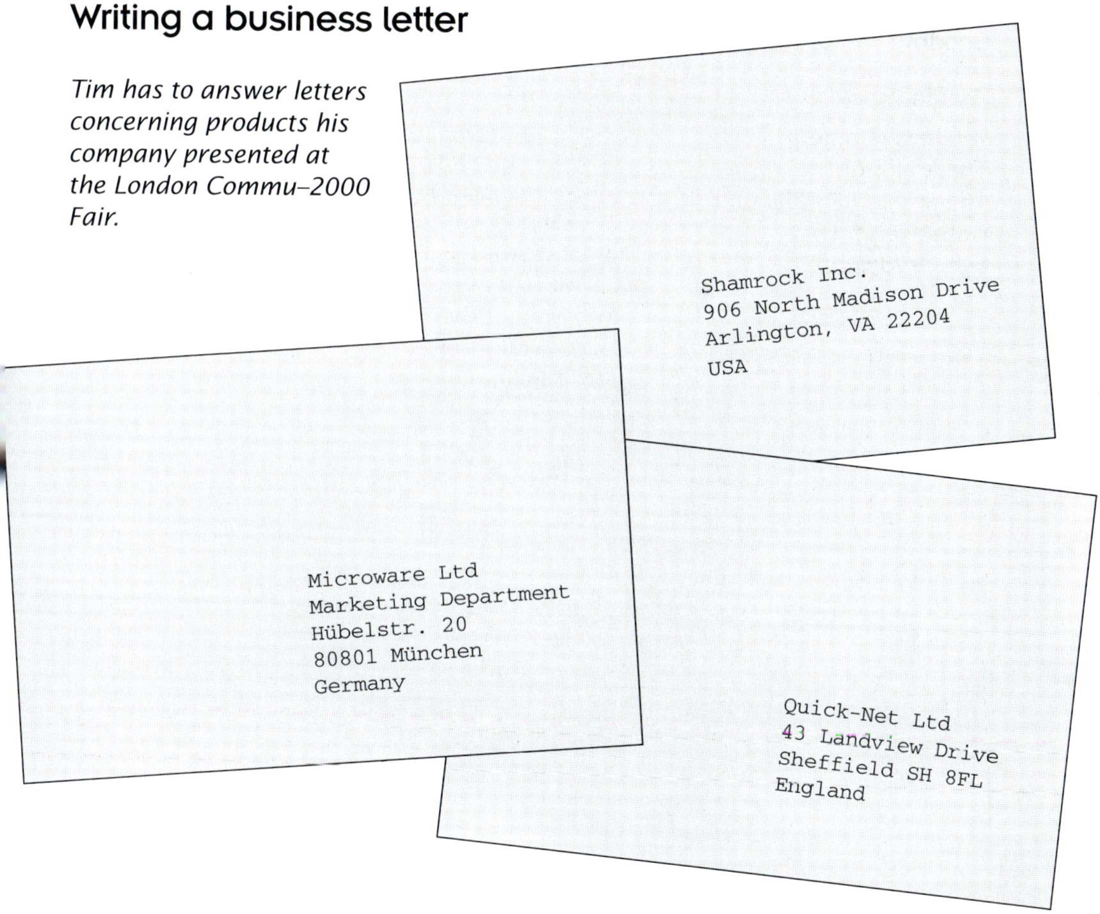

Keep in mind

Arlington, VA 22204 → ZIP code (AE); Sheffield SH 8FL → Postcode (BE)

a **Listen to the cassette. You will hear five addresses. Write them down as if you were addressing an envelope.**

b Match the English/American abbreviations on the left with the German translations on the right.

Example:
3. Sq. – A. Platz

1. St.	A. ~~Platz~~
2. Dept. or Dpt.	B. Nr. 14
3. ~~Sq.~~	C. Postfach
4. No. 14	D. usw./etc.
5. c/o or Attn.	E. vgl.
6. P.O.B. or PO Box	F. Gesellschaft mit beschränkter Haftung
7. etc.	G. zu Händen
8. cf.	H. Postscriptum
9. Ltd	I. so bald wie möglich
10. Corp. (AE)	J. Anlage
11. Inc. (AE)	K. Straße
12. P.S.	L. Aktiengesellschaft
13. enc. or encl.	M. Firma, (die) Herren
14. asap	N. Kapitalgesellschaft
15. Messrs.	O. Abteilung

Keep in mind

Bei den englischen/amerikanischen Abkürzungen (siehe Aufgabe b) gibt es häufig mehrere Möglichkeiten, die gleichermaßen gebräuchlich sind (z.B. P.O.B. oder PO Box, Dept. oder Dpt.).

①

Return address

National-Net Group Inc.

23, rue de Chantelle
75013 Paris
France
Tel.: 1-567241
Téléfax: 1-567238

Address

Microware Ltd
Marketing Department
Hübelstr. 20
80801 München
Germany

Reference(s)

Your Ref.: JG/BD 52
Our Ref.: DK/mn

Date

June 18, 19...

Salutation

Dear Sir/Madam,

Body of letter with reference and reason for writing

We are an international distributor of high speed modems and are looking for an opportunity to do business with Germany in view of the rapidly developing international communications highway. We also supply a wide range of compatible software packages. All our products have been approved by the German Telecom.

Closing sentence

We would appreciate it if you brought our company and its products to the attention of those firms among your customers which are large-scale users.

Complimentary close

Sincerely yours,

Signature (signed and typed)

J.P. Bateau

J.P. Bateau
Marketing Manager

Enclosure(s)

Encl.: Brochure

②

NEDC

18 Funny Side
Pretoria 0002
South Africa

Retu
add

Address

Mr Tim Schneider
Microware Ltd
Marketing Dept.
Hübelstr. 20
80801 München
Germany

20 June 19...

Dat

Salutation

Dear Mr Schneider,

Body of letter with reference and reason for writing

When I attended the Commu-2000 Fair in London, I was impressed with the new Multi-CD your company is distributing in Europe.
As more and more of our customers here in South Africa are showing an interest in this product we are looking for potential suppliers.
We would be most grateful if you could send us a quotation for an initial order.

Closing sentence

We look forward to hearing from you in the near future.

Complimentary close

Yours sincerely,

Signature (signed and typed)

Marc Beaver

Marc Beaver
Sales Manager

Tel.: 0027-12-417-1800
Fax: 0027-12-417-3798

Keep in mind

Wenn nicht bekannt ist, ob es sich bei dem Adressaten um einen Mann oder eine Frau handelt, dann lautet die Anrede *Dear Sir/Madam*.
Die Anrede *Dear Mr Dr Brown* gibt es im Englischen nicht. Stattdessen lautet die Anrede *Dear Dr Brown*. Gleiches gilt für den Titel *Prof.*

Anrede		**Schlussformel**
(*BE*)		
Dear Sir/Madam	→	Yours faithfully
Dear Mr/Ms Brown	→	Yours sincerely
(*AE*)		
Dear Sir/Madam	}	Sincerely yours
Dear Mr/Ms Brown		Very truly yours

Das erste Wort nach der Anrede im Brief (*salutation*) wird immer großgeschrieben.
In einem Geschäftsbrief sind Kurzformen, wie z.B. *it's*, *they're*, *doesn't* usw. nicht üblich.

c Write a suitable salutation and complimentary close for the following addressees.

1. Messrs. Smith & Lowman
2. an unknown addressee
3. Jack and Margaret Camp
4. Dr. Richard
5. a good friend of yours
6. Tina Carter
7. Mike Williams

d Translate Mr Beaver's enquiry (page 40) into German.

e Work in pairs. Complete the enquiry on page 42.
Use the expressions in the box.

Could you please / I was interested / We are a supplier of /as well as
Having visited / there is plenty of demand / we look forward to
We would appreciate it / at the / Dear Sir / offers a wide range / a copy

MEDIA NORM 36, boulevard Hausse
L-2850 Luxembourg

Microware Ltd
Marketing Director
Hübelstr. 20
80801 München
Germany

April 5, 19...

①,

② your stand ③ International Communications Fair in Zürich this year ④ to see that your company ⑤ of some very innovative telecommunication equipment. ⑥ the local government and feel that ⑦ for this type of equipment.
⑧ send further details on your latest models ⑨ the necessary modems. ⑩ if you included ⑪ of your current catalogue.
⑫ an early reply.

Yours faithfully,

Jean Shahir

Jean Shahir
Import Manager

Topic B

Offers

a Work in pairs. Which of these points should always be included when making an offer? Discuss.

1. quality and/or type of goods
2. agency agreement
3. prices and/or discounts
4. sales agreement
5. request for information
6. printed material and/or illustrations
7. delivery date
8. quantity
9. request for quotation
10. terms of delivery and payment

TELEFAX

To: No.: 010 49 869 55903
Firm: Microware Ltd, München, Germany
Name: Mr Georg Schmidt
Dept.: Sales Dept.

From: Hansun Inc., Seoul, South Korea
Name: Hani Yolun
Dept.: Sales and Export
Date: December 4, 19...
Page(s): 1

Dear Mr Schmidt,

We refer to your enquiry of November 30, 19... and are glad to quote as follows:
50 Jet-Print 3x Color $ 350 each. Our prices are all FOB* Seoul, packing included.
If your order is received by the end of December, we can grant you a special end-of-year discount of 2%.
Delivery can be effected immediately from stock. The shipping documents will be surrendered against bank acceptance.
As our prices are expected to rise next year, we would advise you to take advantage of this favorable offer.
Sincerely yours,

Hani Yolun

Hani Yolun
Export Manager

(*FOB or f.o.b. are abbreviations for *free on board*)

b Here is Tim's reply to Ms Shahir's enquiry (page 42). Write the text in the correct order based on the layout of the second letter on page 40.

We look forward to receiving your order / Dear Ms Shahir / We are pleased to send our most recent catalogue with a detailed quotation for the products specified / Encl: catalogue / leaflet / Tim Schneider / 10 April 199... / With reference to your enquiry of 5 April 199... / At this time all models can be supplied from stock / Most of the goods can be supplied with optional modems / All prices include the cost of goods and transport, excluding insurance / Yours sincerely, / Microware Ltd, Munich

c **Work in pairs. Copy the chart and complete the word families.**

Noun	Verb	Adjective (-ing/-ed form)
reference	?	?
?	address	?
?	?	grateful
delivery	?	?
?	supply	?
?	?	competitive
enclosure	?	?
?	enquire	?
?	?	developing
attention	?	?
?	confirm	?
?	?	required
assistance	?	?
?	remain	?
?	?	innovative

d **Translate the following offer into English.**

Sehr geehrter Herr Rodriguez,

wir danken Ihnen für Ihre Anfrage, die Sie an die Zeitschrift Computer Digest gerichtet haben. Anbei übersenden wir Ihnen das gewünschte Prospektmaterial über Universal Adapters und Pocket Adapters.
Sollten Sie noch Fragen bezüglich der Installation und der Anwendungsmöglichkeiten haben, möchten wir Sie bitten, diese an uns zu richten. Unser Außendienst wird Sie dann mit Lösungsvorschlägen unterstützen.
Bei etwaigen Rückfragen stehen wir Ihnen gerne zur Verfügung.

Mit freundlichen Grüßen

Tim Schneider

Tim Schneider

Anlage: Prospektmaterial

Topic C

Orders and delays

a Copy the order form and fill it in. Use the items from the drawing on page 45 to place your order.

Pacific Winds Ltd

14 Campbell St. Pickton SEW 3708 New Zealand

Order No.: LM 4173

Ms Mary McCane
OFF-MAX Office Supplies
526 Kayton Street
Sydney, NSW 2010
Australia

10 August 19...

Quantity	Description of Goods	Unit Price	Total
		Total amount	

Authorized by

. . . .

Tel.: 0064-2-896744
Fax: 0064-2-896755

More detailed and specialized orders are usually written in a letter form. You will find an example of such an order on page 47.

MEDIA NORM

36, boulevard Hausse
L-2850 Luxembourg

Mr Morris Brown
Sales Manager
Microware Ltd
Hübelstr. 20
80801 München
Germany

10 May 199...

Dear Mr Brown,

With reference to Mr Schneider's reply of 16 April and your representative's quotation we would like to place an order for 10 Powermax each with the high speed modem 300-18.2 as well as the OEE 704.3 adapter.
We should be grateful for delivery by 1 June in order to remain competitive in this rapidly developing market. Please confirm that your company can supply these goods by the required date.
We trust that you will give this order your immediate attention and look forward to receiving your prompt acknowledgement.

Yours sincerely,

Jean Shahir

Jean Shahir
Import Manager

b Identify the following phrases in Ms Shahir's letter to Mr Brown.

1. introductory phrase
2. phrase which mentions the order
3. phrase which mentions the delivery date
4. request for confirmation
5. closing sentence

c Your boss has left the following note on your desk. Write the order. The expressions in the box below may help you.

Liebe Frau ...,
bestellen Sie bitte 10 vollautomatische*
Wasserpumpen (Bestellnr. 735SK) mit der
Bitte um sofortige Lieferung und Bestätigung unseres Auftrags.
Vielen Dank!
Mit freundlichem Gruß

B. Wisser

(* fully automatic)

With reference to your quotation ...
We would like to place an order for ...
We are pleased to place an order for ...
We enclose/are enclosing an order for ...
We should be grateful for delivery by ...
We enclose our order for immediate delivery ...
Please acknowledge this order promptly, giving the earliest delivery date ...
Please confirm receipt of this order ...

d Link the sentences (1–5), using an appropriate word from the box.

Example:
He rarely sends letters. A fax is usually cheaper.
He rarely sends letters **because** a fax is usually cheaper.

1. We cannot check this order. We have not checked our stock.
2. We would be grateful for delivery by June 1. We want to remain competitive.
3. We will be able to confirm the order. I have checked our stock.
4. I recently attended the Commu–2000 Fair in London. I was impressed with the new Multi-CD your company is distributing in Europe.
5. Our company needs references. Then we can accept the order.

before
after
because
until
and
when
so that

TELEFAX

To:	No.: 87441926	**From:**	Lights & Things
Firm:	Bulb World	**Name:**	Louis Walley
Name:	William Channy, Assistant Sales Manager	**Dept.:**	Sales Dept.
Dept.:	Sales Dept.	**Date:**	March 8, 19 ...
		Page(s):	1

Ref.: Order No.: EM 6290

Dear Mr Channy,

We have not yet received the order we placed on February 15, 19 ... . In the acknowledgement your company had promised delivery from stock. As there is a great demand for these new energy efficient lightbulbs, we will be forced to obtain the Energy Saver from another supplier if you cannot rush delivery.

Sincerely yours,

Louis Walley

Louis Walley
Assistant Sales Manager

e Role play.
You have just received a customer's fax concerning a delayed order. Your boss asks you to get on the phone and explain why your company has not delivered yet.

Student A: You are the assistant sales manager at Bulb World. Apologize for the delay. The expressions in the box may help you.

> We are/I am very sorry for the delay.
> We/I wish to apologize for ...
> Please accept our apologies for ...
> You'll receive $ ... credit on your next order.

Student B: You are the assistant sales manager at Lights & Things. React to the apology. The expressions in the box may help you.

> We/I clearly stated in our/my order that ...
> We/I must ask you to rush delivery ...
> We/I will hold you liable for any losses ...
> If you don't send ... we/I will be forced/obliged to ...

f Work in groups. Discuss the following question and then report back to the class.

What do you think is more effective: writing a letter, making a phone call, sending a fax, writing a telex, using electronic mail? Give reasons.

g Listen to the cassette. You will hear three recorded messages. Then copy the chart below and fill in the information.

	Offer	Enquiry	Delay in delivery
Details about goods	?	diesel engines	?
Delivery	?	?	?
Prices	?	?	?
Quantity	?	?	?
Terms of payment	?	?	?

Useful phrases

1. Enquiries

Reference to address/advertisement

We owe your address to ...	Wir verdanken Ihre Adresse ...
You have been recommended to us by ...	Sie wurden uns von ... empfohlen.
We have seen your advertisement in ...	Wir haben Ihre Anzeige in ... gesehen.
During a visit to the ... fair, we saw ...	Während eines Besuchs auf der ... Messe, haben wir ... gesehen.

Reason for enquiring

We are looking for ... / We are interested in ...	Wir suchen nach ... Wir interessieren uns für .../Wir sind an ... interessiert.
As we have received many enquiries from our customers ...	Da wir viele Anfragen von unseren Kunden erhalten haben ...
We need/require ...	Wir brauchen/benötigen/haben Bedarf an ...
We are a supplier of ...	Wir sind Zulieferer von ...

Request for information/quotation

Could you please send us ...	Könnten Sie uns bitte ... schicken.
We would appreciate it ...	Wir wären dankbar/würden es sehr schätzen ...
Please inform us/let us know/on what terms you can supply.	Bitte teilen Sie uns mit, zu welchen Bedingungen Sie liefern können.
Please state the earliest date of delivery.	Bitte nennen Sie den frühesten Liefertermin.
Please send us a quotation for ...	Bitte machen Sie uns ein Angebot für ...

2. Offers

Openings

Thank you for your enquiry ...	Vielen Dank für Ihre Anfrage ...
With reference to your enquiry ... / We refer to your enquiry of ...	Wir beziehen uns auf Ihre Anfrage ...
We are pleased to receive your enquiry ...	Wir freuen uns über Ihre Anfrage ...

Prices/discounts

We are pleased to submit our offer.	Wir erteilen Ihnen unser Angebot.
We grant a trade discount.	Wir gewähren einen Händlerrabatt.
Our prices are subject to a discount.	Auf unsere Preise gewähren wir einen Rabatt.
All prices include the cost of goods and transport.	Alle Preise beinhalten Warenkosten und Fracht.

Delivery/payment

Delivery will be effected at the earliest possible date.	Die Lieferung erfolgt so bald wie möglich.
All models can be supplied from stock.	Alle Modelle sind vorrätig.
Cash with order.	Barzahlung bei Bestellung.
Payment on receipt of invoice.	Zahlung nach Erhalt der Rechnung.

Endings

If you have any further questions ...	Sollten Sie noch weitere Fragen haben ...
Should you require any further information ...	Sollten Sie noch weitere Informationen benötigen ...
As prices are expected to rise, we would advise you ...	Da ein Preisanstieg erwartet wird, möchten wir Ihnen raten ...

3. Orders

Openings

With reference to your quotation, we would like to place an order.	Wir beziehen uns auf Ihren Kostenvoranschlag und möchten gerne eine Bestellung aufgeben.
We are pleased to place an order with you.	Wir möchten gerne bei Ihnen eine Bestellung aufgeben.
We enclose/are enclosing our order number.	Wir fügen unsere Bestellnummer bei.
We thank for your quotation of ...	Wir danken Ihnen für Ihr Angebot vom ...

Buyer's instruction/conditions/confirmation

Please confirm receipt of this order.	Bitte bestätigen Sie den Erhalt dieser Bestellung.
Please acknowledge this order.	Bitte bestätigen Sie diesen Auftrag.
This order is subject to our terms and conditions.	Diese Bestellung wird aufgrund unserer Bedingungen erteilt.

Endings

We trust that you will give this order your prompt attention.	Wir hoffen, dass diese Bestellung/dieser Auftrag umgehend erledigt wird.
We look forward to receiving your prompt acknowledgement.	Wir erwarten umgehend eine Bestätigung Ihrerseits.

4. Delays

Reminders/complaints concerning delays in delivery

We must ask you to rush delivery.	Wir müssen Sie bitten, schnell zu liefern.
The long delay is causing us ...	Die lange Lieferverzögerung bringt uns .../verursacht ...
Your company had promised delivery from stock.	Ihre Firma hatte sofortige Lieferung ab Lager versprochen.

Seller's reply

We would like to apologize for the delay.	Wir möchten uns für die Lieferverzögerung entschuldigen.
We offer our sincere apologies.	Wir bitten vielmals um Entschuldigung.
Please accept our apologies for ...	
Owing to a delay in ...	Wegen einer Verzögerung ...

Unit 4

Greeting and accompanying a visitor

Topic A

At the airport

a **Listen to the cassette. Decide if the following statements are true or false. If they are false, correct them.**

1. Mr Thomson had a short but uncomfortable flight.
2. Mr Thomson has got a lot of luggage.
3. Tim helps Mr Thomson to carry his bags.
4. Mr Thomson wants to go to the office first.
5. Mr Thomson's hotel is near Microware.

Tim Schneider: Hello. You must be Mr Thomson. I'm Tim Schneider from Microware. It's a pleasure to meet you. Did you have a good flight?
Mr Thomson: Oh, yes, thank you. A little long, but comfortable.
Tim Schneider: Can I help you with your bags?
Mr Thomson: No, thank you. That's very kind of you but they aren't heavy.
Tim Schneider: My car is in the parking lot. We'll head for the office if that's all right with you. Or would you prefer to go to your hotel first? It's quite near.
Mr Thomson: I would like to go to the office first, really.
Tim Schneider: All right, this way please.

b Work in pairs. Practise meeting a visitor at the airport. Use the flowchart as a guide.

Excuse me, are you ...? My name is ...
Good afternoon, my name's ....
Hello. Welcome to Munich. I'm ...
Hi, how are you?

↘

Yes, I'm ...
Nice to meet you, Ms/Mr ...
Good afternoon, Ms/Mr ...
Fine, thanks. And (how are) you?

↙

How was your flight?
Did you have a good flight?
Was it a long flight?

↘

Long, but very comfortable.
Yes, it was all right. A bit stormy, though.
Yes, it was but I managed to sleep for two hours.

↙

How are things in (New York)?
How's your wife/family?

↘

Everything's fine. Thank you.
They're all very well. Thank you.

↙

How long will you be staying here?
Let me help you with your bags.
Would you like to go to your hotel first?
Would you mind meeting Mr/Ms ... right away?

↘

For (*three days*) only. I have to be back in ... on Tuesday.
Oh, thank you. That's very kind of you.
Yes, that's a good idea.
I'd rather go to the office first.
No, not at all. I am looking forward to meeting her/him.

c Do you know these words? Use your dictionary if necessary.

international flight	departure	trolley
baggage claim	delay	movie
transfer	passport control	cabin crew
domestic flight	check-in	refreshments
arrival	customs	food

Find the opposites of these adjectives.

interesting	comfortable
friendly	wonderful
delicious	bumpy

good	on time
clean	easy
quick	

d Work in pairs. Talk about your last flight. Use as many words as possible from the boxes above.

How was your flight?

It was fine. The cabin crew was very friendly.

What was the movie like?

It was not so interesting.

Topic B

At the office

a **Listen to the cassette. Continue the conversation with Mr Thomson and Mr Brown, the sales manager at Microware.**

Tim Schneider: Here we are. Can I take your coat? Mr Brown will be right with you. Please have a seat. Would you like a cup of tea or coffee?
Mr Thomson: Yes, please. Coffee would be nice.
Tim Schneider: How do you like your coffee?
Mr Thomson: Black with sugar, please.
Tim Schneider: Here you are.
Mr Thomson: Thank's a lot.
Tim Schneider: You're welcome. We've booked you into the Bavaria Hotel just up the road. I hope you'll be happy with your accommodation.
Mr Thomson: I'm sure I will.
Tim Schneider: Oh, here's Mr Brown.

What do you think of our new product?

How are you going to market the product?

Do you think the product is too expensive?

What about delivery? How soon can you deliver?

Keep in mind

Für das deutsche *Bitte* gibt es im Englischen verschiedene Wiedergabemöglichkeiten.

a) auf eine Entschuldigung

Entschuldigung! – Bitte!	Sorry! – That's all right. – It doesn't matter.

b) als Bitte (*please*)

Können Sie mir bitte den Zucker reichen?	Could you pass me the sugar, please?

c) auf Dank

Danke. – Bitte. (Gern geschehen.)	Thank you. – You're welcome. – Don't mention it.

b **Listen to the cassette again. Tim Schneider uses a lot of polite phrases when he speaks to Mr Thomson. List the ones you can remember.**

c **What are Mr Thomson's replies? Add them to your list.**

Tim Schneider	Mr Thomson
Can I help you with your bags?	No, thank you. That's very kind of you, but ...

MICROWARE internal memo

To: *Tim Schneider*
From: *Frank Williams*
Date: *25 September 19 ...*

Tim

Please pick up Ms Jean Wilcock from Chicago at the airport. Arrival tomorrow 2.30 pm, flight TWA 809. If she doesn't want to go to her hotel first (Hotel zur Post), we can meet in my office at 4 pm.
Thanks very much for your help.

Frank

d **Role play.**

Student A: You are Tim Schneider. You pick up Ms Wilcock from the airport. Use as many polite phrases as possible.

Student B: You are Ms Wilcock from Chicago. You meet Tim Schneider at the airport. Use as many polite phrases as possible.

Topic C

Taking a guest out to lunch

Keep in mind

menu - Speisekarte
meal - Menü (Speiseabfolge)
dish - Gericht

starter (BE) }
appetizer *or* hors d'œvre (AE) } Vorspeise

a Work in pairs. Before you listen to the cassette, try to answer these questions.

Ms Anderson is having lunch with Mr Thomson in the restaurant Zum Ochsen.

1. What problems do you think Mr Thomson might have in the restaurant?
2. Which German "restaurant phrases" do you think Mr Thomson might want to know?
3. Which dish on the menu (page 59) might Mr Thomson think is German?

b Listen to the cassette again and answer the following questions.

1. What kind of starters are on the menu?
2. Do they serve any fish?
3. Is goulash a typical German dish?

Ms Anderson: This is one of my favourite places for lunch. It's quite near and they serve excellent food here.

Mr Thomson: I'm sure I'll like it. But it's good to have you with me because my German is miserable. I'm afraid you'll have to help me with the menu. I can't read it.

Ms Anderson: Here we are. This table is reserved for us. Would you like to order a drink first?

Mr Thomson: Yes, I think I'll have a mineral water.

Ms Anderson: And I'll take an orange juice. Herr Ober!

Mr Thomson: How do you call for the waiter in German?

Ms Anderson: You say *Herr Ober*. Now let's have a look at the menu. They have prawn cocktail, tomato soup or hot beef tea as a starter.

Mr Thomson: I think I can do without a starter. I'm not very hungry.

Ms Anderson: As a main course you can choose between fish and meat. All dishes are served with rice, chips, or roast potatoes and veget-ables of the day or salad.

Mr Thomson: What kind of fish do they have?

Ms Anderson: There's rainbow trout and plaice on the menu.

Mr Thomson: And what about meat?

Ms Anderson: The lamb chops are very good. But there's goulash and chicken curry as well. And I can recommend pork fillet or pepper steak.

Mr Thomson: I think I'll have goulash. It's a typical German dish, isn't it?

Ms Anderson: No, not really, but it's very popular in Germany. Well, I'll have the lamb chops. Would you like a beer or do you prefer wine?

Mr Thomson: A beer would be great.

Ms Anderson: We can decide later about the dessert. There's ice cream, mousse au chocolat and a fresh fruit salad. Let's order now. Herr Ober!

The Old Shepherd's Inn

Menu

STARTERS

Soup of the day £2.50
including wholemeal French bread
Garlic Mushrooms £2.50
Smoked Canadian Salmon £3.50
Shrimp Cocktail £3.75

MAIN COURSES

Fresh Pink Salmon £8.95
Sauté Scampi in Herb Sauce £6.50
Veal Cutlet £7.80
Roast Turkey with Cauliflower £7.50
Grilled Lamb Chops with Corn £6.25

All accompanied by salad garnish and potatoes or rice.

DESSERTS

Home-made Chocolate Mousse £2.25
Selection of home-made Puddings £1.95
Fresh Fruit Salad £2.50
Cheese and Biscuits £1.75
Fresh filtered Coffee 80p
Pot of Tea 80p

Tips only accepted if you have fully enjoyed your meal.

Prices include VAT

c You are in a restaurant in Great Britain. Look at the menu on page 61 and tell the waiter/waitress what you would like to have. Use your dictionary if necessary.

Waiter: Can I take your order now?
You: ①
Waiter: And what would you like as a main course?
You: ②
Waiter: I'm sorry, it's off the menu for today. I can recommend the salmon. It's delicious.
You: ③
Waiter: Would you like rice or potatoes to go with that?
You: ④
Waiter: Anything for dessert?
You: ⑤
Waiter: What would you like to drink?
You: ⑥
Waiter: All right. Anything else?
You: ⑦
Waiter: All right. Thank you.

After the meal you ask for the bill.

Waiter: Did you enjoy your meal?
You: ⑧
Waiter: Here you are, that's £22.80.
You: ⑨
Waiter: Thank you very much. Goodbye.

"Order anything you want. I brought $4 with me."

Keep in mind

In Großbritannien, häufig aber auch in Kanada und den USA sind folgende Konventionen in Restaurants üblich:

Ein Schild am Eingang *Wait to be seated* weist darauf hin, dass den Gästen ein Tisch angeboten wird.

Das Fleisch (z. B. *pork*) wird vorher geschnitten. Man isst mit der rechten Hand, die linke ruht auf dem Schoß und nicht auf dem Tisch.

Die Rechnung wird oft unaufgefordert nach Beendigung der Mahlzeit an den Tisch gebracht.

Enjoy your meal entspricht dem deutschen *Guten Appetit*; diese Wendung wird aber selten gebraucht. Bemerkungen während des Essens, wie z. B. *Oh, that's delicious!* sind üblicher.

Es ist ratsam, sich vorher zu informieren, wie viel Trinkgeld erwartet wird. Nicht immer ist die Bedienung im Preis inbegriffen.

d Put the different foods into the right category. Use your dictionary if necessary.

Fruit	Vegetable	Poultry	Fish	Meat	Seafood
		chicken			prawns

lettuce	potatoes	haddock
tomatoes	duck	trout
~~chicken~~	veal cutlet	cabbage
~~prawns~~	steak	beans
beef	kidney pie	peas
pineapple	sole	cod steak
cauliflower	lamb chops	roast beef
turkey	lemon	apple pie
salmon	peach	smoked haddock pie
grapes	cucumber	corn

e Work in pairs.

Student A: Ask your partner the questions (1–7).
Student B: Find an appropriate reply (A–G) to your partner's questions.

What do you say, if ...

1. you don't understand somebody?
2. you are in a restaurant and you would like to pay?
3. you think you have got the wrong bill?
4. you get the wrong dish?
5. you agree with a suggestion?
6. you disagree with a suggestion?
7. you want to recommend some-thing?

A. I'm afraid I have a complaint to make. It's ...
B. Why don't you try the ...? It's delicious.
C. Well, I'd rather ...
D. Oh, yes. That's a good idea.
E. I'm afraid there's something wrong.
F. Sorry, what did you say?
G. Could I have the bill, please?

f Role play *(3 roles).*

You have invited an English friend out for dinner at *The Old Shepherd's Inn*. He or she is a vegetarian, i. e. he or she does not eat meat but accepts fish or eggs. Discuss what is on the menu (page 61) and decide what to take. Order a full meal for two people with a starter, a main course and a dessert.

Topic D

Sightseeing and shopping

a Work in pairs. Read the dialogue with your partner. Then look at the extracts from the list of events on page 65 and complete the missing information.

Mr Thomson is from Chicago. It is his first visit to Munich. So he wants to spend the weekend there, see the sights of the city and do some shopping. While he is having dinner with Ms Anderson at the restaurant Zum Ochsen he asks her some questions.

Mr Thomson: How can I go downtown? Do I have to take a taxi?

Ms Anderson: No, it's easy to get around Munich by underground. Look, this is a map of the underground system and the city centre. Lines 3 and 6 go directly to the centre where most places of interest are. Here is the Marienplatz with the Altes und Neues Rathaus, the town halls. And there is the Liebfrauendom, a beautiful church. If you go along Dienerstraße and Residenzstraße you can see the Residenz on your right and the Feldherrnhalle on your left.

Mr Thomson: I would like to see the exhibitions in the Pinakothek. When is it open?

Ms Anderson: Unfortunately, the Alte Pinakothek is closed due to restauration work, but the Neue Pinakothek is open ① and closed ②. If you're interested in history, you should visit the Residenzmuseum. Opening hours are ③. It's closed on ④. For any further information you can go to the tourist information centre at the main station.

Mr Thomson: That sounds interesting. I'd also like to do some shopping. My boy asked for a T-Shirt from Munich and my wife asked me to bring her a cuckoo clock. For my little daughter I'd like to buy one of those lovely German dolls.

Ms Anderson: Well, you'll get all these things in Neuhauser Straße or Kaufingerstraße.

Mr Thomson: That's wonderful. When do the shops close?

Ms Anderson: They close at 6.30 pm.

Mr Thomson: That's quite different to the States.

Ms Anderson: Yes, I think it is! You'll have to do your shopping first.

Mr Thomson: In the evening I'd like to visit a typical Bavarian beergarden.

Ms Anderson: Oh, yes, this is a must for visitors from abroad. And you have to try our local speciality *Weißwürste*. Have a look at the map. You'll find a very nice beergarden here ...

What's on in Munich?

Neue Pinakothek

Barer Str. 29
Europäische Malerei und Skulptur des 18. u. 19. Jh.
Täglich (außer Mo) 10-17, Di u. Do durchgehend von 10-20 Uhr.
Eintritt 6 DM, So und Fei Eintritt frei.

Stadtmuseum

Sankt-Jakobs-Platz 1
Öffnungszeiten: Di u. Do bis So 10 - 17 Uhr, Mi 10 - 20.30 Uhr
Eintritt 5 DM

Residenzmuseum

Max-Joseph-Platz 3
Fürstliche Räume der Renaissance, des Rokoko und des Klassizismus.
Täglich (außer Mo) 10-16.30 Uhr, Eintritt 5 DM.

Spielzeugmuseum

im Alten Rathausturm, Marienplatz
Sammlung alter europ. u. amerik. Spielsachen aus 2 Jh.
Täglich 10-17.30 Uhr, Eintritt: K 1 DM; E 4 DM

Nationaltheater

Max-Joseph-Platz
Führungen: jeden Freitag um 14.00 Uhr, Karten 5 DM.

Münchner Kammerspiele

Maximilianstr. 26
Do 2.2. 19.00 Uhr
Viel Lärm um nichts
von William Shakespeare
Sa 4.2. 19.30 Uhr
Nathan der Weise
von Gotthold Ephraim Lessing

b Look at the events on this page. What else would you recommend to Mr Thomson? Inform him about opening hours and admission fees. Use your dictionary if necessary.

c Work in pairs.

Student A: You are at the main station in Munich and you would like to visit two churches (Liebfrauendom/Theatinerkirche) and after that meet a friend in the Hofbräuhaus. Ask your partner how to get to these places.

Student B: Look at the map of Munich on page 66 and explain to your partner how to get to the above places.

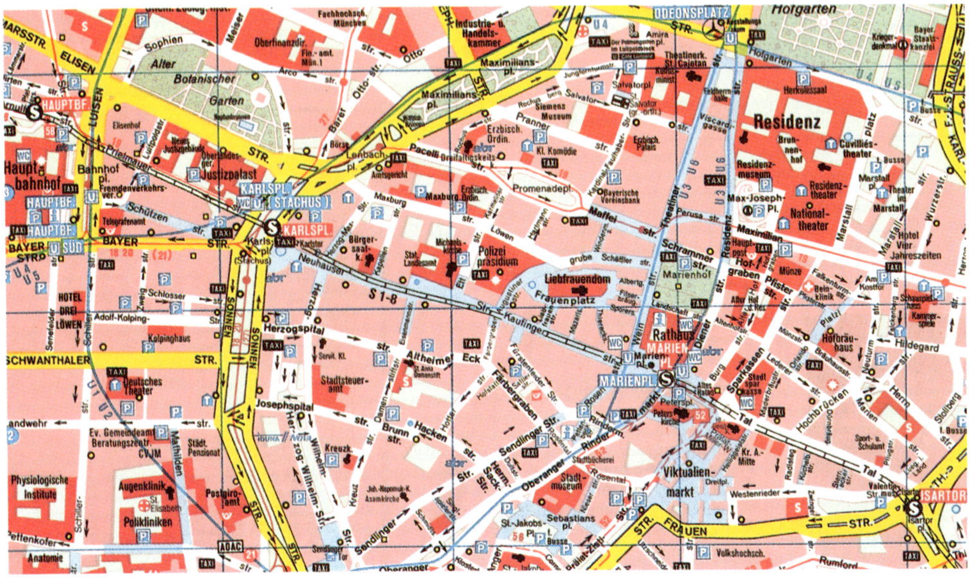

d **Read the following information on the London travelcards on page 66, 67. Use your dictionary if necessary. Then answer these questions.**

1. What are the advantages of a Travelcard?
2. Where can you buy a Travelcard?
3. What kind of Travelcards are available?
4. Do you need a photo for the Travelcard?
5. Is there any price reduction for children?

Travelcards

Travelcards give you the freedom to travel where you choose, as often as you like. The more you use them the better the value, so they're ideal for sightseeing.

No need to hunt for change, no need to ask the fare. Travelcards are affordable and endlessly convenient.

Fares in London are based on a zonal system – just choose the zones you need and you're off.

Travelcards can be bought at Underground stations and at some newsagents.

One Day Travelcard

Use it after 09.30 Mondays to Fridays, any time weekends and holidays.
14 and 15 year olds need a Child-Rate Photocard or must pay adult fares.

Seven Days Travelcard

Use it anytime of the day or night. Adults and children need Photocards.

Photocard

Just take a passport size photo to any Underground station or London Transport Travel Information Centre and pick your photocard up there and then.

One Day Travelcard Prices

	Adult Travelcard	Child Travelcard
Zones 1 & 2	£2.80	£1.50

Travelcard Season Tickets

	Weekly		Monthly		Annual
	Adult	Child (5-15 years)	Adult	Child (5-15 years)	Adult
Zone 1	£11.00	£4.20	£42.30	£16.20	£440.00

(There are other zonal fares and Travelcards available.)

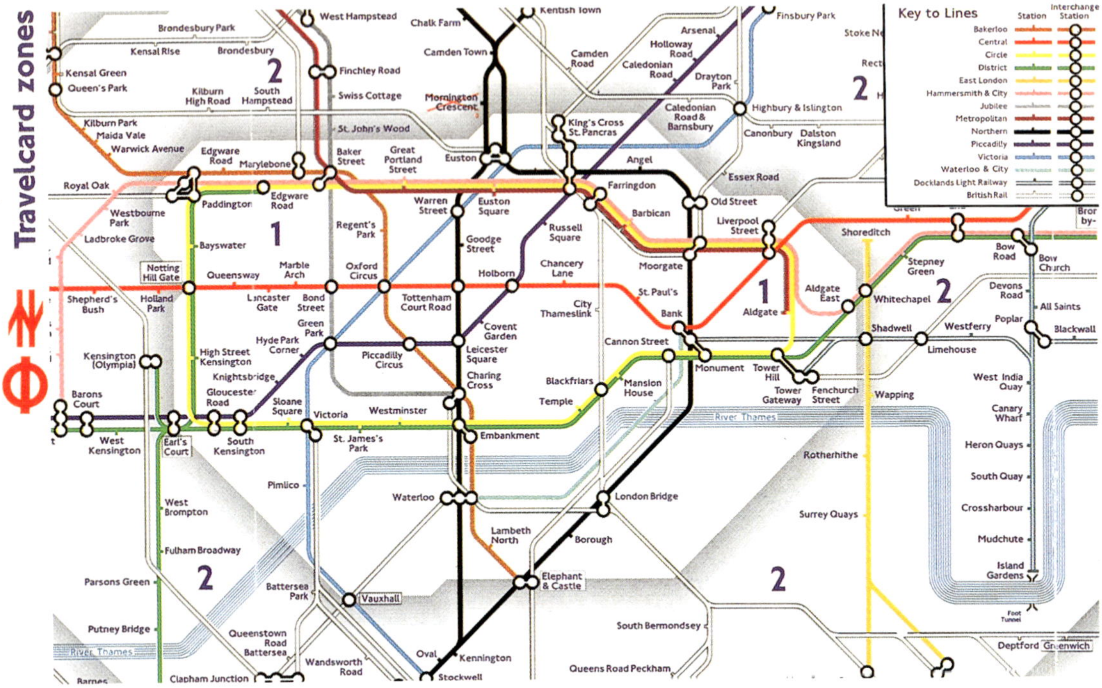

(The Piccadilly Line goes directly to Heathrow Airport.)

e Work in pairs. Look at the map of the London underground system and find your way to the following places.

1. There is a famous fleamarket in the north of London called Camden Lock Market. The underground station is Camden Town. Explain how to get to Camden Town from Victoria Station.

First you take the ...

Take the westbound/ eastbound Circle Line .

You change at ... into ...

You leave the train at ...

2. You have just arrived at Heathrow Airport. You want to go to your hotel near Paddington Station. Which line do you take first? Where do you have to change trains?

3. You want to visit the Tower of London. The underground station is Tower Hill. Your hotel is near Earl's Court in the Southwest of London. How do you get there by underground?

Useful phrases

1. Greeting someone

Nice to see you again.	Schön, dich/Sie wieder zu sehen.
Did you have a good/pleasant/ comfortable trip/journey/flight?	Hattest du/Hatten Sie eine(n) gute(n) /angenehme(n) Reise/Flug?
Can I help you with your luggage?	Kann ich dir/Ihnen mit deinem/ Ihrem Gepäck helfen?
Would you prefer to go to your hotel first?	Möchtest du /Möchten Sie lieber zuerst in dein/Ihr Hotel?
I hope you'll be happy with your accommodation.	Ich hoffe, du wirst mit deiner/Sie werden mit Ihrer Unterkunft zufrieden sein.

2. Offering something

Please, have a seat.	Bitte nimm/nehmen Sie Platz.
Would you like .../What about a cup of coffee/tea?	Möchtest du/Möchten Sie .../Wie wär's mit eine(r) Tasse Kaffee/Tee?
How do you like your coffee/tea?	Wie trinkst du deinen/trinken Sie Ihren Kaffee/Tee?

3. In a restaurant

A table for two, please.	Einen Tisch für zwei Personen bitte.
Could we have the menu, please?	Könnten wir bitte die Speisekarte haben?
Just one more minute, please; we're not quite ready yet.	Einen Augenblick bitte noch; wir sind noch nicht ganz so weit.

4. Ordering a meal

Excuse me, .../Waiter ...	Entschuldigen Sie bitte, .../Herr Ober!
I'd like some ...	Ich hätte gerne ...
We'll start with ...	Wir fangen mit ... an.
Could you bring us some ...?	Könnten Sie uns bitte ... bringen?
I'll have ...	Ich bekomme ...

5. Asking for details

What would you recommend?	Was würden Sie/würdest du mir/uns empfehlen?
What kind of ... have you got?	Was für ... haben Sie?
Do you have a house wine?	Haben Sie einen Hauswein?

I'm afraid I don't know what ... means. Could you tell me what it is?	Es tut mir Leid, ich weiß nicht, was ... bedeutet. Können Sie/Kannst du mir sagen, was das ist?
Is it fish/meat/vegetable/soup?	Ist es Fisch/Fleisch/Gemüse/Suppe?
What is the best wine of the region?	Was ist der beste Wein aus dieser Region?

6. Possible answers

It's not that easy to explain.	Das ist nicht so leicht zu erklären.
It's hard/difficult to explain.	Es ist schwer zu erklären.
It's a sort of .../It's a kind of .../It's a bit like ...	Es ist so etwas wie .../Es ist so ähnlich wie ...
I'm sorry, but I don't know the English word for it.	Es tut mir Leid, aber ich weiß nicht, wie das auf Englisch heißt.
This is a speciality of the region.	Das ist eine Spezialität dieser Region.

7. Paying

Could I have the bill, please?	Könnte ich bitte die Rechnung haben?
Could we have separate bills, please?	Könnten wir bitte getrennte Rechnungen haben?

8. Asking for information

When is/are ... open?	Wann ist/sind ... geöffnet?
Do you know where I can get/buy ...?	Weißt du/Wissen Sie, wo ich ... bekommen/kaufen kann?
Where can I rent a car?	Wo kann ich ein Auto mieten?
How much is a taxi to ...?	Was kostet ein Taxi nach ...?
Where is the nearest underground station?	Wo ist die nächste U-Bahn-Station?
Is there a (regular) bus service from ... to ...?	Gibt es eine Busverbindung von ... nach?
Where can I change money?	Wo kann ich Geld umtauschen?

Unit 5

Planning a business trip

Topic A

Booking a flight

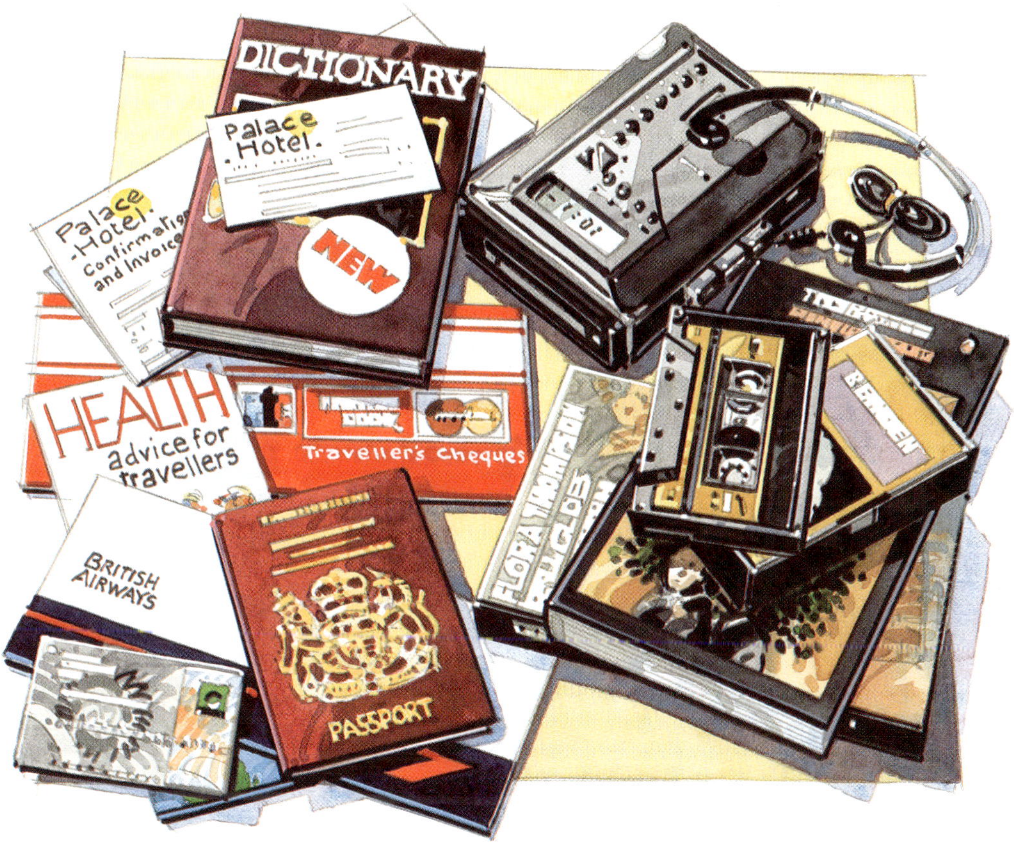

a **You are planning a business trip abroad. Write down ten things you might want to take with you. You can choose objects from the picture above.**

b **Work in pairs. Compare your list of things with your partner's. Ask your partner why he or she has chosen the items on his or her list. Report back to the class.**

c Listen to the cassette. Make notes on the following questions.

1. How many people are flying to Boston?
2. Why are these people going to Boston?
3. Why does Miriam decide to fly from Frankfurt and not from Munich?

d Work in pairs. Read the dialogue with your partner. Then check your answers to the questions (1–3).

Angela: Nelson's Travel. Guten Tag.
Miriam: Hello, Angela. This is Miriam Tellmann from Microware in Munich. How are you?
Angela: Hello, Miriam. Fine, thanks. And you?
Miriam: I'm fine, too, thanks. Two colleagues and myself are flying to Boston for the fair and I would like to book three return flights from Munich to Boston.
Angela: Oh, lucky you! When would you like to leave?
Miriam: We would like to be in Boston on May 2nd.
Angela: And when would you like your return flight?
Miriam: On May 8th, please.
Angela: There are no direct flights from Munich to Boston. You would have to change planes in New York. Or you could fly from Frankfurt. There is one direct flight from Frankfurt to Boston daily.
Miriam: Yes, I think Frankfurt would be better.
Angela: Okay. Let me see what's available. Which class would you like?
Miriam: Business class, please.
Angela: Yes, I have three flights on May 2nd, but I'm afraid the Boston - Frankfurt flight on May 8th is full. Flights are available either on May 7th or on May 9th.
Miriam: May 9th would be better, I think.
Angela: Good. You fly out of Frankfurt at 10.20 am. Check-in is an hour earlier. So I'll book you on the 8.05 flight from Munich.
Miriam: When do we arrive in Boston?
Angela: You arrive in Boston at 12.10 pm local time. There is a six-hour time difference.
Miriam: And what about the return flight?
Angela: You leave Boston at 6.15 pm arriving in Frankfurt at 9.55 am on May 10th. The connection to Munich is no problem. There is a flight at 10.45 am.
Miriam: That sounds good.
Angela: Okay. I'll make the booking.
Miriam: Thanks a lot for your help.
Angela: You're always welcome. Have a good trip!
Miriam: Thanks, bye.

Keep in mind

Das Datum

Geschrieben:	Gesprochen:
May 2nd, 1995 May 2, 1995 May 2, '95	May the second, nineteen ninety-five
2nd May(,) 1995 2 May '95	The second of May, nineteen ninety-five
2.5.95	the second of the fifth, ninety-five

e Role play.

Student A: You work for a travel agency. A customer (Student B) will ask you for information about planes from Frankfurt to Tokyo. Study the information below and use it to answer the questions.

From Frankfurt to Tokyo

Flight No.	Dep. time	Arr. time (Local Time)
LH 710	13.30	8.45
FU 577	14.50	12.30 (with stop in Moscow)
NH 210	19.40	14.55
JL 408	20.50	16.10

1. Lufthansa (LH) flights depart from Terminal 5, Aeroflot (FU) depart from Terminal 2; All Nippon Airways (NH) depart from Terminal 3; Japan Airlines (JL) depart from Terminal 1
2. Check-in time on all international flights: 60 mins before departure

Student B: You want to find out about flights from Frankfurt to Tokyo. You go to a travel agency and ask the assistant (Student A) for the following information:

- the time of the first plane to Tokyo
- the arrival time
- if there are any other flights in the late afternoon
- the terminal numbers for these flights
- the check-in time for these flights

f Work in groups. What are your experiences of these aspects of travelling?

Topic B

Booking a hotel room

a Work in pairs. Read the dialogue with a partner.

Tim calls Mary O'Neill in Boston to make hotel reservations for the fair.

Mary O'Neill: Good morning. Mary O'Neill speaking.
Tim Schneider: Good morning, Ms O'Neill. This is Tim Schneider from Microware in Munich. I phoned you a couple of weeks ago about a reservation for a stand at the fair in spring.
Mary O'Neill: Oh, yes. I remember. I received your confirmation about a week ago. Is there anything wrong?
Tim Schneider: No, nothing at all. I'd like to make hotel reservations for myself and two of my colleagues. Could you possibly help me?
Mary O'Neill: Yes, I think so. How long are you going to stay?
Tim Schneider: We arrive in Boston May 2nd and return to Munich May 9th.

Mary O'Neill: That will be for seven nights then. Would you like single or double rooms?
Tim Schneider: Three single rooms with bath, please.
Mary O'Neill: Hold the line a moment, I'll find out for you. I have three single rooms with bath at the Regent Hotel in downtown Boston. There is a good bus service to the fair. Would that be okay?
Tim Schneider: That sounds very good. How much are the rooms?
Mary O'Neill: They are $110 per night.
Tim Schneider: Does that include breakfast?
Mary O'Neill: No, it doesn't. But there is a hotel restaurant in the lobby.
Tim Schneider: Great! Could you reserve the rooms for us, please?
Mary O'Neill: Yes, of course. I'd need your credit card number, then.
Tim Schneider: Right. It's ... Thank you very much. Goodbye.
Mary O'Neill: You're welcome. Goodbye.

b Decide if the following statements are true or false. If they are false, correct them.

1. Mary O'Neill cannot remember speaking to Tim Schneider.
2. She received the confirmation of Microware's reservation for a stand at the fair about a week ago.
3. Tim Schneider calls Mary O'Neill to get information on hotels in Boston.
4. Tim Schneider is travelling to Boston with three colleagues.
5. They are going to stay in Boston for ten nights.
6. Tim Schneider asks for three single rooms with bath.
7. The Regent Hotel is outside Boston.
8. The rooms cost $115 per night, including breakfast.

c Role play.

Student A: You have to book rooms for your colleagues who are going on a business trip. Ring up the hotel to make the booking. Ask for the following rooms:

- a single room with bath/shower from June 1st to June 5th
- a double room with bath for 10th June
- two single rooms with shower and a double room with bath/shower from June 22nd to June 26th

The following examples may help you.

I'd like a single/double room.

Is breakfast included?

I'd like a room with bath/shower.

How much is the room per night?

Could I book the conference room on June 2nd from 8 am till 12 pm?

Student B: You are the hotel clerk. Look at your notes below and find out if the required rooms are still available. The following examples may help you.

The room costs … per person/a day.

Breakfast is (not) included.

The room's got a bath/shower.

I'm afraid we're fully booked.

All rooms have got TV and telephone.

Friday, 2 June
Conference rooms no. 2 and no. 3 booked all day
Sunday, 4 June
All single rooms full
Saturday, 10 June
Two double rooms with shower left
Thursday, 15 June
Conference rooms booked all day
Friday, 23 June
All single rooms with bath booked
Saturday, 24 June
All double rooms with shower booked
Costs:
Single rooms with $70 and with $85 per night
Double rooms with $90 and with $120 per night

d Work in groups. Look at the list of hotel facilities. Reach an agreement on the five most important facilities for somebody on a business trip.

- hourly bus service to the fairgrounds
- heated swimming pool
- fully-equipped modern conference room
- 24-hour room service
- all rooms with bath
- all rooms with telephone services
- boutiques, hairdresser in the lobby
- IDD (international direct dialling) phones
- cocktail bar
- 24-hour coffee shop
- free car parking
- fitness centre with sauna
- secretarial services including translations
- hotel restaurant
- fax and photocopying machines

e **Work in pairs. Imagine that you are designing a business hotel. You can choose between a first- and a middle class hotel. Consider the location and the facilities you would like to offer. Present your ideas to the class.**

Topic C

Buying a train ticket

a **Work in pairs. Read the dialogue with your partner and then listen to the cassette. Is it the same? Make notes of any differences you notice.**

Clerk: Good morning, Madam. Can I help you?
Passenger: Yes, please. I'd like a return ticket from London to Liverpool.
Clerk: Would that be first or second class?
Passenger: Second class, please.
Clerk: Would you like to reserve a seat?
Passenger: Yes, I have to be in Liverpool by 2.30 pm tomorrow and would like to return on the first train back to London the next day.
Clerk: Okay. All right. Would you like an aisle or a window seat?
Passenger: Window seat, please.
Clerk: Is that smoking or non-smoking?
Passenger: Smoking, please.
Clerk: Good. I've booked you on the 12.45 train to Liverpool tomorrow morning. The first train from Liverpool to London is at 5.25 am. They go every hour.
Passenger: Oh, well, in that case I think the 7.25 train will be early enough.
Clerk: Right you are, Madam. Here you are. Here is your ticket and your reservation. Have a good trip!
Passenger: Thank you very much and goodbye.

b **Listen to the cassette again. How many differences did you find? Practise the dialogue with your partner.**

c **Role play.**

Student A: You want to travel from London to Paris by the Channel Tunnel. You go to the railway station and ask for the following information:

- the time of the first train to Paris
- the arrival time in Paris
- if it is necessary to reserve a seat
- the platform number the train leaves from
- the station the train arrives at

Student B: You work as a clerk at the railway station. Use the information in the box to answer Student A's questions.

Trains from London (Waterloo/Intel Station/ Platform 1) to Paris (Gare du Nord) using the Channel Tunnel. Reservations required for all seats.	
Dep. time	**Arr. time**
07.23	11.24
12.53	16.54
16.23	20.24
16.48	20.57
17.48	21.57

"Probably the logo for the new high-speed Channel Tunnel link."

d Match the two halves of these sentences.

1. If you phone him now, ...
2. If you book early, ...
3. You will have a good connection, ...
4. If you do not ask him to come with us for lunch, ...
5. If it is 11 am in London, ...
6. We will take a double room, ...
7. I will have to stay overnight, ...
8. If we fly to New York, ...

A. he ... disappointed (be)
B. if there ... any single rooms left (not be)
C. you ... the hotel you want (get)
D. ... if I cannot get a flight home.
E. he ... in his office (be)
F. we ... change airports (have to)
G. if you ... to Amsterdam (fly)
H. it's 8 pm in Tokyo

e Translate into English.

1. Wenn wir früh wegfahren, kommen wir rechtzeitig (*in time*) an.
2. Wenn ich keinen Rückflug mehr bekomme, muss ich in New York übernachten.
3. Wenn mein Zug Verspätung hat, komme ich zu spät zur Konferenz.
4. Wenn du am Mittwoch nach München kommst, werde ich dich zum Abendessen einladen.
5. Wenn wir länger in Boston bleiben, können wir uns die Stadt ansehen.

Topic D

Travel problems

"This is your captain speaking ...
I apologize for the bumpy ride.
We are now flying about ten feet ...
Mr Tatlow's had a go ... who's next?"

a **Listen to the cassette. Make notes on the following questions.**

1. Where does Frank Williams want to travel to?
2. Why is he going there?
3. How long will it take Frank Williams to get to the company in Berlin from the train station?
4. Which train would he like to take back to Munich?
5. What type of seat does Frank Williams ask for?

b **Work in pairs. Read the dialogue with your partner and compare each other's answers to the questions (1–5).**

Tim Schneider: Tim Schneider speaking.
Frank Williams: Good morning, Tim. This is Mr Williams. Could you do me a favour, please? I have to go to Berlin for a meeting tomorrow at 4 pm. I want to take the train. Could you pick up the ticket for me at the station?
Tim Schneider: Sure, Mr Williams. You have to be in Berlin at 4 pm?
Frank Williams: Yes, and it will take about a quarter of an hour by taxi to get to the company from the station.
Tim Schneider: When will you be returning to Munich?
Frank Williams: I'd like to be on the first train out of Berlin the next morning.
Tim Schneider: First or second class?
Frank Williams: I'd like a first class, non-smoking, aisle seat, please.
Tim Schneider: Fine, Mr Williams. I'll bring you the ticket when I get back.
Frank Williams: Thanks Tim, that's a great help.
Tim Schneider: You're welcome.

c **Listen to the cassette. Make notes on the information given. What do you think Mr Williams will do in this situation?**

d You are going on a very important business trip. What will you do if ...

- you miss your flight?
- you loose your luggage?
- your seat on the flight has been double-booked?

Example:
If I miss my flight, I'll ...

e Work in pairs. Write down travel problems you or people you know have had. Tell your partner about them.

1. Lost luggage
2. Missed connection
3. Visa not valid
4. Bad weather
5. Train cancelled
6. Passport expired
7. Ticket forgotten
8. Become ill
9. Money and travel documents stolen
10. Bomb threat at the airport

f Role play.

Student A: You are on a business trip when you are suddenly faced with a problem. Phone your business partner and explain to him or her what has happened.
The following phrases may help you.

I'm afraid	I've missed the plane. I've lost my luggage. I've forgotten my ticket. the weather is so bad that all flights have been cancelled. etc.

Student B: Listen to your partner's problems and find out what he or she is going to do. Maybe you can make suggestions to help.
The following phrases may help you.

Why don't you ...?
What about ...?
How about ...?
You could ...?

Useful phrases

1. Booking a flight

Passenger

I'd like to fly to ... next week/on ...	Ich möchte gern nächste Woche/am ... nach ... fliegen.
Business/tourist/first class, please.	Business class/Touristenklasse/ 1. Klasse, bitte.
How much is a single/return ticket to ...?	Was kostet eine einfache Fahrkarte/ Rückfahrkarte nach ...?
Could you book me on the next flight to ...?	Könnten Sie den nächsten Flug nach ... für mich buchen?
Is that a direct flight?	Ist das ein Direktflug?

Travel agent

Would you like a single/return flight?	Möchten Sie einen einfachen Flug/ Rückflug?
Which class would you like to fly?	In welcher Klasse möchten Sie fliegen?
That's ... (money)	Das macht ...
I'm sorry, but that flight is fully booked.	Es tut mir Leid, aber dieser Flug ist ausgebucht.
You must change planes in ...	Sie müssen in ... umsteigen.

2. Booking a hotel room

Guest

I'd like a single/double room.	Ich hätte gern ein Einzel-/Doppelzimmer.
I'd like a room with bath/shower/ WC.	Ich hätte gern ein Zimmer mit Bad/ Dusche/WC.
I will be staying for two nights/one week.	Ich bleibe zwei Nächte/eine Woche.
I've booked a single/double room for two nights.	Ich habe ein Einzel-/Doppelzimmer für zwei Nächte reserviert.
How much is the room per night?	Was kostet das Zimmer pro Nacht?

Hotel clerk

How long are you planning to stay?	Wie lange wollen Sie bleiben?
I'm afraid we're booked up.	Wir sind leider ausgebucht.

Would you fill in the registration form, please?	Könnten Sie bitte das Anmeldeformular ausfüllen?
The room costs ... per night.	Eine Übernachtung kostet ...
Here's your key, Madam/Sir.	Hier ist Ihr Schlüssel.
Enjoy your stay!	Einen angenehmen Aufenthalt!

3. Buying a train ticket

Passenger

I'd like a single/return ticket to ...	Ich hätte gern eine Fahrkarte/Rückfahrkarte nach ...
How much is a 1st/2nd class ticket?	Was kostet eine Fahrkarte erster/zweiter Klasse?
When does the train leave?	Wann fährt der Zug?
When is the next train to ...?	Wann geht der nächste Zug nach ...?
When does the train arrive?	Wann kommt der Zug an?
Do I have to change trains?	Muss ich umsteigen?
Is that a direct train?	Ist das eine Direktverbindung?
Which platform does the train leave from?	Auf welchem Bahnsteig fährt der Zug ab?
Is there a buffet car on the train?	Hat der Zug einen Speisewagen?
Are there sleeping coaches on the train?	Hat der Zug Schlafwagen?

Clerk

A single or a return ticket?	Eine einfache oder eine Rückfahrkarte?
Would you like 1st or 2nd class?	Möchten Sie erster oder zweiter Klasse fahren?
Smoking or non-smoking?	Raucher oder Nichtraucher?
Would you like compartment or single seating?	Großraum oder Abteil?
You have to change trains at ...	Sie müssen in ... umsteigen.
Would you like to reserve a seat?	Mit oder ohne Platzreservierung?

Unit 6

On a business trip

Topic A

Arriving in Boston

Tim Schneider, Patricia Newman and Miriam Tellmann have arrived in Boston to represent Microware at the PC World Fair.

a Work in pairs. How good is your memory? Try to remember the things which were done to prepare this trip. Decide if the following statements are true or false. If they are false, correct them.

1. Miriam reserved two stands for the fair by telephone.
2. The bigger stand was reserved for Electro Sul.
3. Patricia booked the flights, arriving in Boston on May 2nd and returning from Boston on May 8th.
4. Tim booked the hotel rooms through a German travel agency.

b Listen to the cassette. Make notes on the following questions.

Tim, Patricia and Miriam are checking in at their hotel.

1. How many rooms have been booked for them?
2. What is the problem with the booking?
3. Is there a solution to the problem?
4. Are their rooms next to each other?
5. Where does the shuttle bus to the fair leave from?
6. Where must they get the tickets for the bus?

c Put the different hotel services into the right category. Some of the services could go in both categories. Use your dictionary if necessary.

room service
~~conference rooms~~
~~hairdresser~~
fitness centre
cocktail bar
coffee shop
~~swimming pool~~
~~fax facilities~~
sauna
photocopying facilities
flower shop
restaurant
translation service
tennis courts
cable TV in every room
interpreter service
early morning calls
computer rental service
car rental service
city tours
all rooms with balcony
massage service
typing service
bureau de change
courier service
laundry and dry cleaning service

Business	**Pleasure**
conference rooms fax facilities	hairdresser swimming pool

d Work in pairs. Compare your lists. Discuss any differences of opinion.

Examples:
Room service could also be useful for business, if you have an all-night work session in your room.
Computer rental could also be useful for pleasure, because some people like to relax by playing computer games.

e Match the hotel guest's questions and problems (1–12) with the hotel clerk's answers and solutions (A–J).

Hotel guest's questions and problems:

1. You would like to know how early you can have breakfast.
2. You would like to know when dinner is served.
3. You would like to know how late the bar stays open.
4. You would like coffee sent to your room in the early morning.
5. You would like to use the sauna.
6. You would like to rent a car.
7. You need to change some marks into dollars.
8. You have to send a fax to your home office.
9. You need photocopies of some documents.
10. You need to get a coffee stain removed from your jacket.
11. You have to get up at 5.30 am the next morning.
12. You need a taxi immediately.

Hotel clerk's answers and solutions:

A. There is a fax machine and a photocopier in the communications room in the lobby.
B. You can place an order for an early-morning call with the reception.
C. The hotel restaurant is open from 7.30 to 11.30 am for breakfast and from 6.00 to 9.30 pm for dinner.
D. The telephone number for the car hire service is 427 9856.
E. The reception can order you a taxi in seconds.
F. The hotel bar is open from 6.00 pm until 2 am. "Happy Hour" (with reduced prices) is from 6.00 to 7.00 pm.
G. There is a currency exchange at the reception desk (24-hour service).
H. The swimming pool and sauna are open from 7.00 am until 10.00 pm.
I. The hotel offers a 24-hour laundry service and a 2-hour express dry cleaning service (from 9.00 am to 4.00 pm).
J. Room service is available 24 hours a day. Just phone the reception desk.

Keep in mind

currency exchange (AE)
bureau de change (BE) – Wechselstube

f Role play.

Student A: You are a guest at the hotel. Phone the reception from your room and ask the clerk for information or advice. Start with the questions and problems in the box above, then use some ideas of your own.

Student B: You are the hotel clerk at the reception. You receive a call from one of the guests who has a question or a problem. Use the answers and solutions from the box above to help the guest or use ideas of your own.

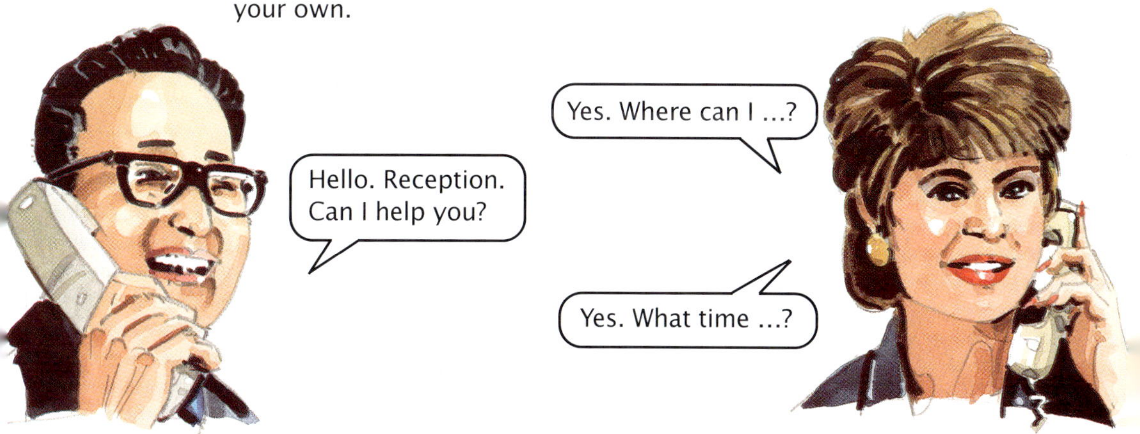

Topic B

At the Boston Trade Fair Centre

The PC World Fair starts tomorrow morning. Final preparations are being made. Tim, Patricia and Miriam are at the exhibition hall to check their stand and to attend the official press conference. Tim meets Carlos Lopez from Electro Sul, who has the stand next to Microware. Carlos is having some problems.

a Work in pairs. Read the dialogue with your partner.

Tim Schneider: Good evening, Mr Lopez. How are you?

Carlos Lopez: Well, I'm a bit nervous. Our flight was late and we didn't get here until late this afternoon. Most of our hardware was shipped to New York by mistake. It only arrived here about an hour ago. So our software demonstrations haven't been checked yet. And only half of our brochures have been delivered. The rest will be sent here tomorrow. Is everything OK with your stand?

Tim Schneider: Yes. We came straight here from the airport at lunchtime to set things up. All our stuff was delivered safely. Our stand was ready within three hours. Then we went to check in at the hotel and freshen up. Miriam and Patricia have a couple of things to do before we go to the press conference.

Carlos Lopez: I'm impressed. You seem to be very well organised! Not like us!

Tim Schneider: Well, I represented Microware at the COMMU-2000 Fair in London last year and at the International Communications Fair in Zürich a few months ago. So I'm accustomed to the routine by now.

Carlos Lopez: Did you have any problems the first time?

Tim Schneider: Oh yes! When we arrived in London, we discovered that our rooms at the hotel had only been booked for one night! And all of our brochures had been sent to Birmingham. That was a mess!

Carlos Lopez: Oh dear! Well, I hope we will be better prepared next time.

b Look at all the sentences in the dialogue which are made with parts of the verb *to be*.

Some of them describe a "state".	*Examples:* I'm a bit nervous. Our flight was late. You seem to be very well organized.
Others describe an "action" or "event". These are "passive" sentences, in which we do not know or are not so interested in who did it.	*Example:* Most of our hardware was shipped to New York by mistake.

c Work in pairs. Identify and write out all the "passive" sentences in the text. Do not write out the "state" descriptions.

d Now transform the sentences into "active" forms. Use "somebody" as the subject.

Examples:
Most of our hardware was shipped to New York by mistake.
Somebody shipped most of our hardware to New York by mistake.

e Work in pairs. Transform the sentences (1–8) into the passive, to put the main emphasis on the words in bold type. If you think it is necessary to mention the person who did it, you can do this with "by + person" at the end of the sentence.

Examples:
We have reduced **the prices of our software.**
The prices of our software have been reduced.

The managing director represented **Microware** at the conference.
Microware was represented at the conference by the managing director.

1. We will send **the documents** to you tomorrow.
2. They deliver **all their goods** from stock.
3. The secretary is typing **the report** right now.
4. Someone at the hotel stole **my passport.**
5. Electro Sul has developed **a new telecommunications system.**
6. When we arrived, someone had already set up **our stand.**
7. He cannot find **the documents.**
8. The manager must sign **all order forms.**

f This is one of the press releases which was issued at the press conference. Read it and decide if the following statements are true or false. If they are false, correct them.

1. The largest category at last year's show was Software, Consulting and Services.
2. Over half of the stands at the fair are for software suppliers.
3. Software suppliers will be showing older versions of their programmes.
4. In the future, more and more people will work from home.
5. "Software for Europe" is a programme for use in offices.

PRESS

PRENSA IMPRENSA ПРЕССА PRESSEN مطبوعات PERS الصحافة STAMPA BASIN प्रेस PRESSE 報道 LEHDISTÖ ΤΥΠΟΣ 新聞稿

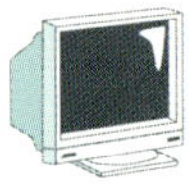

PC World Fair '95
B O S T O N
May 1995

Growing range of software products

Software, Consulting and Services will be the largest category at this year's exhibition, continuing the trend of recent years. Altogether some 1,640 software suppliers are represented at the fair. The total number of exhibitors in all categories is more than 5,500 firms and organizations from over 50 countries.
As well as many updated versions of older programs with new features, software suppliers will be promoting a wide range of innovative developments and specialized solutions in the fields of telecommunication and multimedia for both homes and offices.

Welcome to the digital office!
In the future, more and more businesses will use networks of desktop computers with customized software systems. And with the development of the information superhighway and fast modem technology, more and more people will become teleworkers, communicating from home by video-conferencing. Documents will increasingly become multimedia packages with pictures, sounds and video as well as text, numbers and graphs.
At the special exhibition "Software for Europe" visitors can find out about the latest European programs suitable for various types of business.

Further information for the press: Please contact Mary O'Neill, Tel.: Boston 001 617 330 1067.

g Find the following words in the text and then match them with the correct definitions.

1. range	A. right for the purpose
2. exhibition	B. designed exactly for one particular user
3. trend	C. someone who shows their product at a fair
4. exhibitor	D. a variety
5. feature	E. a movement in a particular direction
6. promote	F. try to make something popular
7. customized	G. someone who does not travel to work
8. teleworker	H. an aspect or quality
9. suitable	I. a place where things are shown to visitors

h Work in groups. Choose one of the following topics and discuss it. Talk about the *positive* and the *negative* aspects of the topic. Can you think of further topics?

Future Developments in Computer Technology

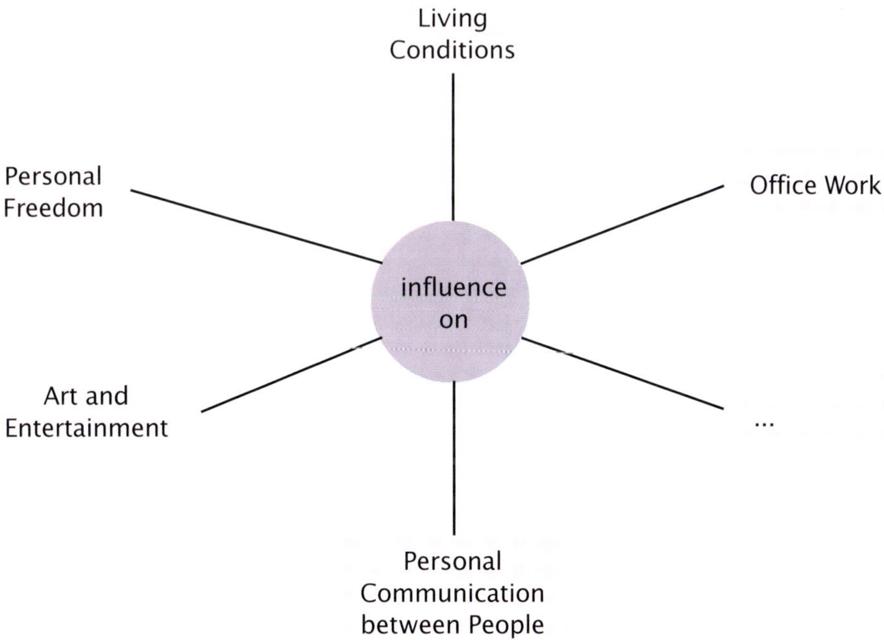

Topic C

Making business contacts

The PC World Fair

a Read the following text about trade fairs and exhibitions, then use words from the text to complete the sentences below the text.

Trade fairs and exhibitions

One of the most popular and effective ways for producers to display and promote their new products is the international trade fair or exhibition. This is usually an annual event held at a major centre.
Brochures, free samples and discussions with representatives of companies on their stands offer potential customers and the general public insights into latest trends and new developments. For people working in the same sector fairs offer a chance to meet and to compare their product ranges.
Representatives have to be able to mix business and pleasure, because successful socializing is often the first step towards new contracts and increased turnover. In Europe this may involve social drinking, while alcohol is not usually allowed on stands at shows in the USA.

1. Our latest model is on ? at our stand over there.
2. We have an ? meeting of all cooperating companies every September.
3. If you like, I can give you a ? of the product, and you can try it out for yourself.
4. According to our survey, the ? market for this new product in South America is very large.
5. The reception after the conference was a chance to ? with the representatives of the other companies.
6. Business is good! Our ? has increased by 20% this year.
7. Excuse me, Sir. I'm afraid you are not ? to smoke in here.

b Read the following dialogues with a partner.

Tim, Patricia and Miriam are busy dealing with enquiries at the Microware stand.

Miriam: Good afternoon. Can I help you?
Customer: Yes. I'm interested in your range of high speed modems.
Miriam: Well, this is our most popular model, the 300-18.2. It's selling very well on the European market at the moment.
Customer: Mmm. Have you got a brochure about it?
Miriam: Yes, here you are.

Customer: Excuse me. I'd like some information about universal adaptors.
Patricia: Yes. We distribute a large selection of adaptors. Can I give you a copy of our catalogue?
Customer: Thank you. Are they suitable for use with portable hardware?
Patricia: Well, the pocket adaptors are. We have some on display over here.

Tim: Can I help you, Sir?
Customer: Could you tell me something about the Powermax?
Tim: Certainly. We have a demonstration model over here.
Customer: What does it cost?
Tim: The unit price is $1500 but we offer discounts for large orders.
Customer: And what about delivery?
Tim: We deliver from stock, so it's relatively fast. How many units would you be interested in?

c Role play. You may use language from the dialogues (page 91).

Some Microware products:
- the Multi-CD (multimedia business software)
- the Micromax (compact portable hardware)
- the OEE 704.3 universal adaptor (for connecting different hardware systems)
- the Ultrafax (telecommunications equipment)
- ...

Student A:
You are visiting the fair and are interested in a Microware product.

Ask the Microware representative

↓

for information about the product/ for a brochure/for a catalogue

↓

to show you the product/to give you a demonstration/to give you a sample

↓

about prices and discounts/about delivery

Student B:
You are representing Microware at the fair. Deal with the potential customer's enquiries.

You can

↓

give information about the product/ offer a brochure/a catalogue

↓

show a model/give a demonstration/give a sample

↓

give information about prices and discounts/give information about delivery

d Work in groups. Read the instructions and play the game.

START

- Introduce yourself. Say something about your company.
- Ask the others who they are and which company they work for.
- Ask one of the others if the fair has been a success.
- Go back one square.
- Talk about your company's best-selling product.
- Talk about what you normally do in your company.
- Ask one of the others about their hotel in Boston.
- Go back one square.
- Ask the others when they are going home.
- Ask one of the others if they would like another drink.
- Go back one square.
- Give the others your telephone number in Germany.
- Tell the others you have to go. Say goodbye and …

FINISH

INSTRUCTIONS

You are at the "end-of-the-fair" reception for all the representatives and you are standing with some people you haven't met before.

Toss a coin to move. Heads = two squares; tails = one square. Follow the instructions in the square and start conversations. The others in the group *must* join in the "role play". The first to reach the finish is the winner.

Topic D

Checking in at the airport

Tim, Patricia and Miriam are on their way home after the PC World Fair. They are at the airport, checking in for their flight back to Germany.

a Work in pairs. Read the dialogue with your partner.

Check-in agent: Good evening. May I see your tickets, please?
Patricia: Here they are. The three of us would like to sit together if possible.
Check-in agent: Would you like smoking or non-smoking?
Patricia: Smoking, please.
Check-in agent: I have two seats together in row twenty and one seat behind them in row twenty-one, smoking section. Do you have any luggage to check in?
Patricia: Yes, we have these four suitcases.
Check-in agent: And do you have any hand luggage?
Patricia: No, we don't.
Check-in agent: Okay. The airport security charge is $10 each.
Patricia: That's $30 altogether. Here you are.
Check-in agent: Thank you, Madam. Here are your tickets. The baggage claim check is attached to the back of each ticket. And here are your boarding cards. Boarding time is at 8.15 at gate 7. Enjoy your flight!
Patricia: Thank you. Goodbye.
Check-in agent: Don't forget your boarding cards!

b Now listen to the cassette. Is it the same? Make a note of any differences you hear. Compare your notes with those of your partner. How many differences did you find? Read the dialogue together again and make some more changes.

c **Work in pairs. Here is a list of things people usually do at airports before their plane takes off. Put them in the right order.**

A. have a cup of coffee
B. go to your gate
C. show your boarding card
D. buy some things at the duty-free shop
E. check in for your flight
F. watch the departure display for boarding information
G. pay airport security charge
H. buy a book or a newspaper
I. check in your luggage
J. board the plane
K. read the departure display for check-in information
L. find your seat
M. write and send off some last postcards to friends at home
N. go through passport control
O. go to your check-in desk
P. go to the departure lounge
Q. get your boarding card
R. fasten your seat belt
S. make sure your luggage is clearly labelled
T. watch the planes taking off and landing

d **Most items in the list above are "obligatory". You have to (you must) do them. Make sentences with *You have to .../You must ...***

e **Five items in the list above are not "obligatory". You can do them if you want, but you don't have to (you needn't). Make sentences with *You don't have to .../You needn't ...***

There are a lot of strict regulations at airports:

- Passengers must check in 60 minutes before departure on international flights.
- Passengers must have a valid passport for international flights.
- Passengers must not take more than one piece of hand luggage onto the plane with them.
- Passengers must not carry dangerous articles like compressed gas containers, fireworks, explosives, etc. in their luggage.
- Passengers must not leave their luggage unattended at any time.
- Passengers must not smoke during take off and landing.
- Passengers must not use radio telephones or other electronic devices which may interfere with the plane's electronic equipment.

f **Fill in the gaps in these sentences with *mustn't* or *needn't/don't have to.***

1. It's an international flight, so we ? forget to take our passports.
2. The flight from Boston to Washington is a domestic flight, so we ? show our passports.
3. The plane to Hawaii departs at 11.30 am, so we ? arrive at the airport later than 10.30 am or we'll be too late for the check-in.
4. You ? take out travel insurance for the flight, but it's better to be safe than sorry.
5. It's still two hours until the plane takes off, so we ? go through passport control yet. Let's go for a coffee first. This place is cheaper than the one in the departure lounge.
6. You ? use that radio telephone in here! It might interfere with the plane's radar and we might crash.
7. You ? take your eyes off your flight bag for a moment. Someone could put a bomb or some drugs in it while you're not looking.
8. You ? keep checking the board for information. They'll announce it over the loudspeakers when the flight starts boarding.

g **Translate into English.**

1. Ich darf nicht vergessen die Fahrkarten morgen zu bestellen.
2. Das Hotel war ganz in der Nähe des Messezentrums, also mussten wir nicht weit gehen.
3. Die Verträge werden bis morgen früh übersetzt.
4. Könnten Sie mir etwas zum Preis und Mengenrabatt sagen?
5. Diese neue Software wurde von unserer Forschungsabteilung entwickelt.
6. Sie dürfen im Hotelzimmer nicht kochen.
7. Es tut uns Leid, aber Ihr Gepäck ist verloren gegangen.
8. Wir werden ganz früh aufstehen müssen, wenn wir rechtzeitig am Flughafen ankommen wollen.

Useful phrases

At the fair

Customer	
I'm interested in ...	Ich bin an ... interessiert.
Have you got a brochure about ...?	Haben Sie einen Prospekt über ...?
I'd like some information about ...	Ich hätte gerne ein paar Informationen über ...
Are they suitable for ...?	Eignen sie sich für ...?
Could you tell me something about ...?	Könnten Sie mir bitte etwas über ... sagen?
What does it cost?	Was kostet das?
What about delivery?	Wie steht es mit der Lieferung?
Sales staff	
Can I help you?	Kann ich Ihnen helfen?
It's selling very well.	Es verkauft sich sehr gut.
We distribute a large selection of ...	Wir vertreiben eine große Auswahl von ...
Can I give you a copy of our catalogue?	Darf ich Ihnen einen Katalog mitgeben?
We have ... on display over here.	Wir haben ... hier drüben ausgestellt.
We have a demonstration model over here.	Wir haben ein Vorführmodell hier drüben.
The unit price is ...	Der Stückpreis beträgt ...
We offer discounts for large orders.	Wir geben Mengenrabatt.

Unit 7

Applying for a job

Topic A

Job advertisements

① Be part of our global expansion!

We are looking for someone special to join our team in Frankfurt.

The successful applicant will have a business background, preferably in the computer industry, to become part of our marketing team. His/her tasks will include assisting our marketing director, arranging meetings, planning and organizing presentations at fairs and keeping our customers informed on the development of new products as well as working with and contacting other national and international companies.
This is a great opportunity for a young, energetic, hardworking and flexible person who is willing to travel.
Accept this challenge and send your résumé and cover letter to:

NetCom, Inc.
Mainstraße 128
60325 Frankfurt

We are an equal opportunities employer.

② Industrial

Sales opportunity.

A division of a Fortune 500 manufacturer, established in 1919, has overseas opening. Extensive training, stable market, repeat business, high independence, full benefits, management opportunity with relocation. Please send your CV to:

Maggie Rath
Regional Recruiting Manager
CHEMWORLD
90 Royal Square
London W5R 3LB
England

③ Local Car Dealership

Seeking full-time experienced office worker, computer-literate, accounts receivable, accounts payable and warranties desired. Great benefit package: major medical, dental, paid vacation, excellent working conditions.
Send résumé to:

Jonesboro Motors
509 Belmore Street
Charlotteville NC 30041
USA

Tourism ④

Needed immediately!

We have an opening for a hardworking person who has good "people skills". If you are ambitious, open-minded and have the desire to become one of our top travel agents apply in writing to:

Outlook Travel
30 Albion Street
Birmingham B2 7SC
England

a Why do you think the first ad appeals to Tim? What are the requirements? Copy the chart and fill it in.

Job-requirements	Personal qualities
	energetic

b Work in pairs. Look at the ads 1–5 and decide which job you would apply for. Give reasons.

> I'd prefer ad no. 4 because I enjoy working with people.

Logistics ⑤

The world of logistics is still growing. That's why we need you at the centre of our operations. An international forwarding agent in search of a clerk with skills, such as operating a workstation, handling documents, basic knowledge of English and Geography.
If you think you can handle the pressure of this type of business send your CV to:

GET
103, boulevard Wilson
L-2850 Luxembourg

c Work in groups. Look at the following list of standard information given in a CV. What other information would you also give?

- Your name, address and telephone number
- Your date of birth
- Your marital status
- Your hobbies and free-time activities
- Details of all the jobs you have had
- Details of training courses you have attended

Preparing a CV

Before preparing a CV, you need to make a list showing your educational background in chronological order as well as a complete list of all the jobs you have had. (This chronological order should always be used when talking about work experience.) You should start with your most recent position.
After you have established this list including the dates of employment and the names of supervisors, you need to analyse exactly what experience you have that might be of interest to your potential employer, i.e. adapt your CV to the position you are applying for.
After completing your list you make a similar list of any other activities you have taken part in and which have allowed you to develop leadership capacities, and to demonstrate initiative and organizational skills. You should analyse these activities in the same way you analysed your jobs.
Keep the job advertisements in mind and match as many of your skills as possible to the job profile.
Preparing a CV as a student or an apprentice is a difficult task because of the lack of professional experience.

d Answer these questions on the text.

1. In which order should all the jobs be listed?
2. What important information should be included in the list?
3. Why are other experiences important to mention?
4. Which decision has to be made before including all job experiences in a CV?
5. Why is it more difficult for a student or an apprentice to write a CV?

Topic B

Job descriptions

a Describe the skills/activities shown in the pictures (1–6). Use suitable words from the box.

Example:
Selling computer disks. (*first picture*)

assisting	filing	planning	record keeping
computing	issuing	preparing reports	scheduling
coordinating	launching	processing	~~selling~~
developing	organizing	programming	taking inventory
directing	ordering	purchasing	working in teams

b Look again at the verbs in exercise a. Match them with the words given below. Some words can be used more than once.

a computer / a sales campaign / new equipment / from an overseas company / monthly expenses / a new sales strategy / a marketing campaign / a department / a company / a meeting / company products / team work / ~~a staff meeting~~

Example:
Scheduling a staff meeting.

c Work in pairs. Ask your partner which of the skills in exercise a he or she has used on the job. Then your partner will ask you.

d Think of additional skills which you might want to include in a CV.

dealing with foreign correspondence

organizing presentations

chairing a meeting

giving product information

e Match the job titles (1–14) on the left with the ones (A–N) on the right.

1. office employee/clerk	A. Reisekaufmann/frau
2. typist	B. Personalleiter/in
3. receptionist	C. Referent/in für Öffentlichkeitsarbeit
4. administrative assistant	D. Versicherungsvertreter/in
5. travel agent	E. Spediteur/in
6. computer operator	F. Marketingfachmann/frau
7. marketing representative	G. Verkäufer/in
8. sales assistant	H. Computerfachmann/frau
9. sales representative	I. Büroangestellte/r
10. insurance salesman/-woman	J. Fachkraft im Flugscheinverkauf
11. public relations assistant	K. Verwaltungsangestellte/r
12. personnel manager	L. Schreibkraft
13. ticket agent	M. Herr/Dame am Empfang
14. forwarding agent	N. Vertreter/in

Keep in mind

Bei Personenbezeichnungen wird im Englischen zwischen männlichen und weiblichen Vertretern der Gattung unterschieden.
Das geschieht bei Berufsbezeichnungen durch Wortpaare mit unterschiedlichen Formen (z.B. *-man/-woman*, wie in *salesman/saleswoman*), seltener durch spezielle Nachsilben, wie in *host/hostess, actor/actress* usw.
Es gibt darüber hinaus eine sehr umfangreiche Gruppe von Berufsbezeichnungen, die sowohl für männliche als auch für weibliche Vertreter gelten.
Zusätze in Form von *man/woman*, *male/female* werden oft dann gemacht, wenn Frauen in Berufen auftreten, die als typisch männlich gelten und umgekehrt (z.B. *female politicians*, *a woman professor*, *a male nurse*).
Im Zuge der Emanzipation der Geschlechter werden bestimmte geschlechtsunterscheidende Personenbezeichnungen durch geschlechtsneutrale ersetzt, z.B. *chairperson* statt *chairman*.

Topic C

Curriculum Vitae

a Work in pairs.

Student A: Study Tim's CV.
Student B: Ask questions based on the information given in Tim's CV.

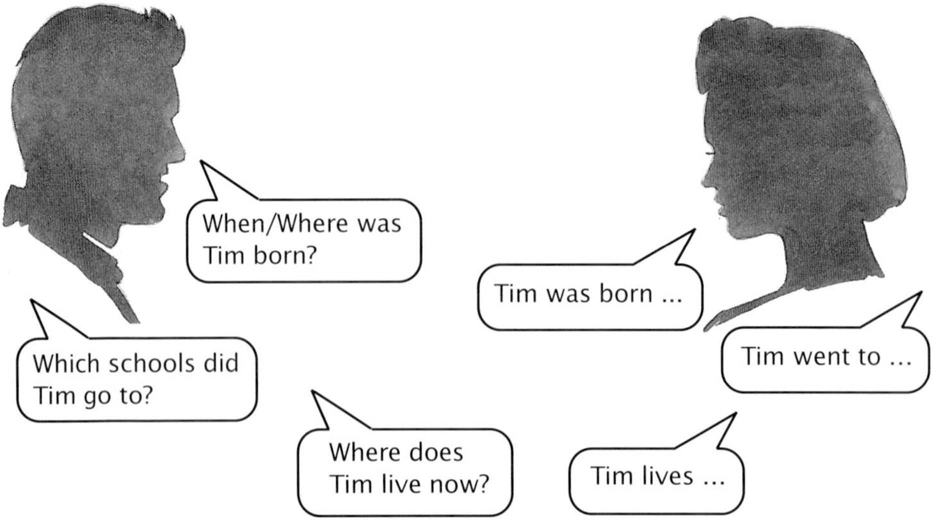

Curriculum Vitae

Personal

Name:	Tim Schneider
Address:	Leopoldstraße 8a 80802 München
Tel.:	(089) 8938062
Date of Birth:	September 14, 1974
Place of Birth:	Düsseldorf, Germany
Nationality:	German
Marital Status:	Single

Education

1980 – 84:	Primary School (Grundschule Unter den Linden, Düsseldorf)
1984 – 90:	Secondary School (Wissmann Realschule, Düsseldorf)
1990 – 91:	Springfield High School, Illinois, USA (exchange student)

Work Experience

1991 – 94:	Apprenticeship in industrial office management at C-Base, Düsseldorf
Training in:	record keeping accounts receivable customer service sales and marketing
1994:	Microware Ltd, München
Position:	Marketing assistant
Responsibilities:	help to organize a telemarketing programme write individualized customer proposals interpret statistical data related to the present market coordinate marketing efforts develop future marketing plans organize in-house meetings make company travel arrangements for fairs

Other Qualifications

Languages:	English: very good knowledge French: fair working knowledge

Good computer skills

Other Activities	Volunteer work with youth groups Tournament table tennis

Curriculum Vitae

Personal

Name:	René Martin
Address:	Willmannstr. 165 10782 Berlin
Tel:	(030) 4769233
Date of Birth:	13 February 1973
Place of Birth:	Karlsruhe
Nationality:	German
Marital Status:	Single

Education

1979 – 83:	Primary school
1983 – 89:	Secondary school (Realschule)
1989 – 90:	Business school (Berufskolleg)

Work Experience

1990 – 92:	Apprenticeship in industrial office management
1992 –	Marketing trainee with Office World (Stuttgart)

Responsibilities

contacted companies and organized presentations of new products
evaluated customer needs
established written estimates
prospected clients by mail and phone

Other Qualifications

Computer:	Good knowledge of software on IBM compatibles Word/Excel
Languages:	good working knowledge of English near native fluency in French

Keep in mind

CV = curriculum vitae (BE); curriculums oder curricula vitae (pl.)
Résumé (AE)

b Compare the two candidates Tim and René. Who do you think is more qualified for the position of marketing assistant? Give reasons.

Examples:
I think Tim is more qualified because he had training in sales and marketing.
No, I believe René is more qualified because ...

c Now it is your turn to write your own CV.
Use a word processor or typewriter to produce your final draft.

The State School System in Great Britain

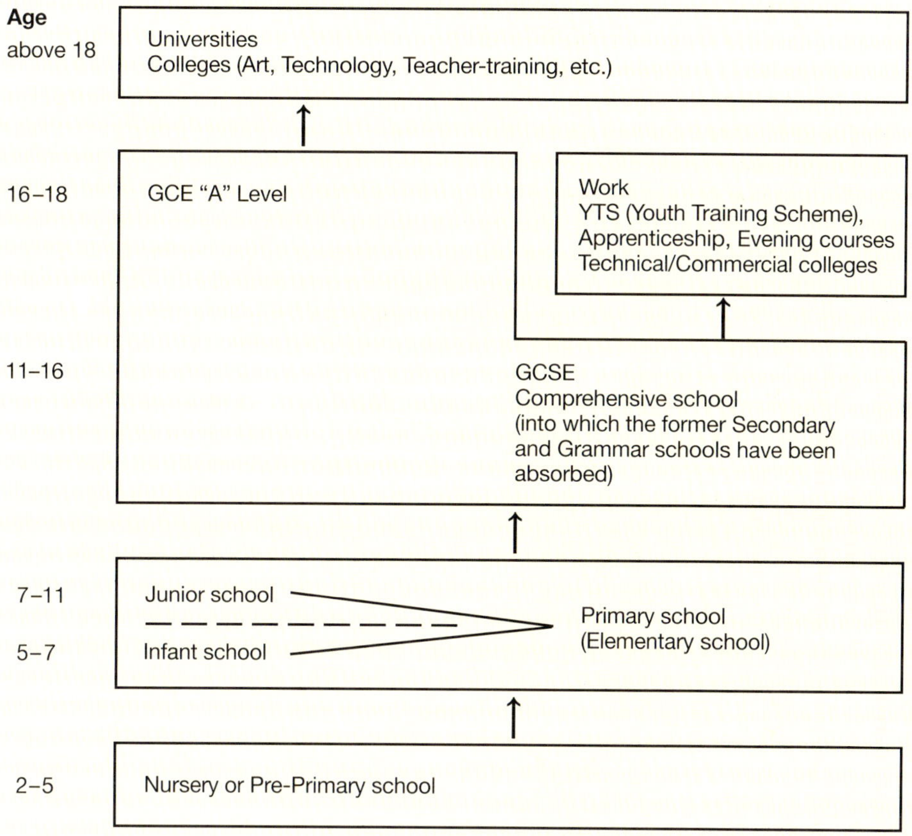

d Work in pairs. Look at the two diagrams (pages 105, 106) and answer these questions before you listen to the cassette.

1. At what age does compulsory education begin in each country?
2. How long does a child have to go to elementary school in France and Great Britain?
3. When does compulsory education end in each country?
4. When do pupils take their first big exam in Great Britain?
5. Why do pupils in France take exams at the end of their four years at college?

e Listen to the cassette and check your answers to the questions (1–5).

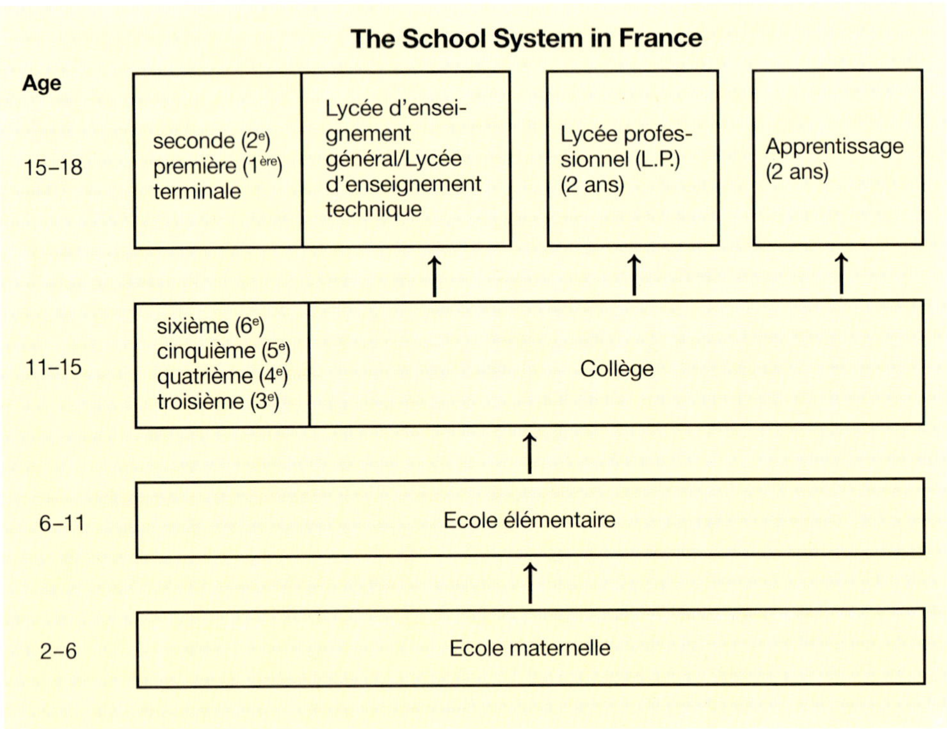

f **Work in groups. Compare the two school systems to the German one and discuss advantages and disadvantages. Make notes and report back to the class.**

Topic D

A letter of application

a **The words in the box describe the different parts of Tim's letter of application. Match the words (A–J) with the numbers (1–10) in Tim's letter.**

Example:
A. salutation – Dear Mr Artner (4)

A. ~~salutation~~	D. return address	H. complimentary close
B. conclusion	E. date	I. introductory paragraph
C. professional experience	F. educational details	J. signature (typed and signed)
	G. addressee	

Tim Schneider
Leopoldstraße 8a
80802 München (1)
Tel. (089) 8938062

June 12, 199... (2)

Jack Artner
Personnel Director
(3) NetCom, Inc.
Mainstraße 128
60325 Frankfurt

(4) Dear Mr Artner,

(5) Please find the enclosed résumé in response to your advertisement offering a position in marketing, which was advertised in the Süddeutsche Zeitung on Saturday, June 9,199...

(6) My marketing background includes a three-year apprenticeship with C-Base in Düsseldorf, where I received training in developing new sales territory.
This involved helping to recruit, train and work with the salesforce. I was also part of a team which developed and implemented sales and marketing plans and strategies in support of the field sales team for Central and Eastern Europe.

(7) I am presently employed as marketing assistant for Microware, software distributor in Munich. However, I am very eager to return to a full range computer service company. In my present position I call in and service merchandisers, retail chains and department stores.

I have achieved success in these and other related activities. I am a result-oriented person who enjoys travelling and working with people.

(8) Enclosed please find my résumé which indicates in some detail my training and experience. I sincerely hope that my qualifications are of interest to you and that an interview might be arranged at your convenience.
Thank you for your consideration and I look forward to hearing from you soon.

(9) Sincerely yours,

Tim Schneider

(10) Tim Schneider

b Write the German version of Tim's letter.

c Christy Reed has just dictated the following letter into a dictaphone. Write a proper letter of application. Pay attention to style, layout, capitalization and punctuation.

dear sir or madam as a graduate from the London school of economics I am interested in obtaining an entry level accounting position with your company you will see from the enclosed résumé I maintained a good grade average throughout my years in college majoring in accounting and minoring in economics for the past three summers I have been employed as a temporary accounting clerk by personal inc my assignments included working with several known agencies in the advertising industry I will call early next week to set up an appointment for an interview I am confident that I have the qualifications to become an asset to deely and johnson ltd yours truly christy reed

Useful phrases

1. Offering a position

We have an opening ...	Wir bieten Ihnen eine Stelle ...
Seeking ...	Wir suchen ...
Local company needs ...	Ortsansässige Firma sucht ...
We are looking for ...	Wir suchen nach ...
Join our team!	Kommen Sie zu uns!

2. Describing qualifications

As you will see from the enclosed résumé ...	Wie Sie aus dem beigefügten Lebenslauf ersehen können ...
I am presently employed as ...	Ich bin derzeit als ... beschäftigt/tätig.
In my present position as ...	In meiner derzeitigen Stelle als ...

3. Responses to job offers

I am interested in obtaining the ...	Ich bin an der ... interessiert.
I wish to apply for the post of ...	Ich möchte mich auf die Stelle als ... bewerben.
I am applying to your advertisement of ...	Ich bewerbe mich auf Ihre Anzeige vom ...
Enclosed please find ...	Anbei/In der Anlage finden Sie ...
I enclose a copy of my curriculum vitae.	In der Anlage finden Sie meinen Lebenslauf.
I would appreciate your consideration.	Über eine Einladung zu einem Vorstellungsgespräch würde ich mich freuen.

Unit 8

A job interview

Topic A

Invitation to the interview

NetCom, Inc.
Mainstraße 128
60325 Frankfurt
Tel.: 069/61 79 53
Fax: 069/61 25 87

Tim Schneider
Leopoldstraße 8a

80802 München

3 July 199...

Dear Mr Schneider,

Our personnel department has received your letter of application and CV for the position of marketing assistant in response to our advertisement in the "Süddeutsche Zeitung".

We are pleased to schedule an interview for you on 3 August 199... at 2pm at our Frankfurt office.

We would appreciate it if you could confirm the date as soon as possible.

Yours sincerely,

Caroline Devon

Caroline Devon

pp.
Personnel Department

Tim is excited about the invitation and phones the company to confirm the date of the interview.

a Work in pairs. Read the dialogue with your partner. Then make a list of all the examples of polite English in the conversation. Compare your list with your partner's.

Receptionist:	NetCom. Ms Miller speaking. Can I help you?
Tim Schneider:	This is Tim Schneider. May I speak to someone in the personnel department?
Receptionist:	Certainly, just a moment, please. I'll put you through.
Tim Schneider:	Thank you, Ms Miller.
Ms Mackey:	Personnel department, Ms Mackey. Good afternoon.
Tim Schneider:	This is Tim Schneider. I'm calling to confirm my appointment for an interview with Mr Artner.
Ms Mackey:	That's very kind of you, Mr Schneider. Could you please confirm your appointment in writing.
Tim Schneider:	Of course. Would it be all right if I faxed it?
Ms Mackey:	Yes, that would be fine.
Tim Schneider:	Thank you, Ms Mackey. I'll try to send it off today.
Ms Mackey:	Thank you very much, Mr Schneider. Goodbye.
Tim Schneider:	Goodbye.

TELEFAX

To:	No. 069/612587	**From:**	Tim Schneider
Firm:	NetCom, Inc.		Leopoldstr. 8a
Name:	Jack Artner, Personnel Director		80802 München
Dept.:	Personnel Department	**Date:**	3 July 199...
		Page(s):	1

Dear Mr Artner,

Thank you very much for considering my application and providing me with a chance for an interview.

I herewith confirm the date and time of my interview, 3 August 199... at 2pm.
I look forward to meeting you in Frankfurt.

Yours sincerely,

Tim Schneider

Tim Schneider

b Match the words (1–10) on the left with the words (A–J) on the right.

Example:
confirm (1) – verify (D)

1. ~~confirm~~	A. opportunity
2. chance	B. staff
3. job interview	C. regarding
4. application	D. ~~verify~~
5. personnel	E. written request for a job
6. considering	F. questioning a person for employment
7. providing	G. supplying
8. schedule (v.)	H. get
9. response	I. plan (v.)
10. receive	J. reply (v.)

c You have been invited to a management training programme. Write a letter accepting the invitation. Follow the structure as shown in the grid. The phrases in the box below may help you.

Opening paragraph	I am writing to confirm receipt of your letter ...
Body of letter	I am very pleased to accept this offer and ...
Closing paragraph	I will contact your office for more details ...

writing to confirm/receipt of letter/management training programme/proud to have been selected/pleased to accept/will contact for more details/thank you for the offer/consideration/Yours sincerely

Keep in mind

I am writing to confirm receipt of your letter ... ist ein sehr formeller Stil; denkbar wäre auch eine neutralere Formulierung, wie z.B. *Thank you very much for your invitation ...*

Topic B

The day of the interview

a Describe Tim in the above photos. The adjectives in the box may help you.

1. What does he look like?
2. How is he dressed?
3. What will he wear for the interview?

Example: (fourth picture)
Tim is wearing an elegant business suit. He looks very ...

sloppy	professional	happy
~~elegant~~	self-confident	friendly
casual	shy	optimistic
sporty	insecure	ambitious
well-dressed	reliable	relaxed
smart	funny	dynamic
properly-dressed	cheerful	

b Work in pairs. Which of the adjectives in exercise a do you think are *positive* and which do you think are *negative* qualities? Sort them into two lists and discuss them with your partner.

c Work in groups. Describe your "perfect" female applicant.

Example:
She is wearing a two-piece suit with a silk blouse and shoes with medium-sized heels. She is friendly and ...

What makes a good interview?

d Look at the pictures (1–4) and find some things that should be avoided in an interview.

e Work in pairs. What factors do you think are important in an interview situation? Make notes and compare them with your partner's.

f Use the words from the box to complete the text.

During the interview show self confidence. Greet the (1) in a sincere and (2) manner and introduce yourself with a (3) handshake. First (4) are extremely important. They include (5) communication such as body language, (6) contact and (7) quality. Sit up (8) against the back of the chair with an (9) and interested expression. Keep arms (10), hands (11) quietly on the chair or in your (12).

resting	impressions
straight	friendly
lap	firm
nonverbal	eye
voice	alert
interviewer	relaxed

Everyone's guide to a job interview

1. "Tell me about yourself."

Talk about job-related skills, in particular those which would be useful in this particular job. Do not ask the interviewer to clarify his or her question. Personal, academic or job-related experience is fine as long as it is related to your potential job performance.

2. "What do you know about this position and the company?"

If you haven't done any research at this point you are dead. Don't forget that it is as important to research the position as it is to research the company.

3. "Why do you want this job?"

Be honest. Use your research/information as well as your own assessment of your skills and experiences as they relate to the position.

4. "What are your strengths? What are your weaknesses?"

Make specific and full statements. Think of the skills checklist (Unit 7) that you used to write your CV.

5. "Where do you see yourself in five years?"

Rely on your research about the organization to describe how you plan to develop your skills within the typical career ladder of the organization. Avoid identifying goals that will not interest the employer.

6. "We have interviewed ten candidates who are as qualified as you are. Why should we choose you over the others?"

Again, the most powerful information you can offer is to emphasize your best skills for the job. Keep in mind that your enthusiasm and desire for the job are also very important.

7. "Do you have any questions?"

Prepare questions ahead of time. Your questions reflect the quality of your research and the clarity of your thinking. Good questions are an excellent way to sell yourself.

8. "What salary are you looking for?"

Do not ask about the salary during the initial interview. If you can, try to delay discussions until the employer is convinced that he or she really wants to hire you. If your interviewer insists, you should have a good idea of an appropriate salary range because of your research on the position.

g Work in pairs. Look at *Everyone's guide to a job interview* (page 114). How would you answer the questions? Make notes and roleplay the interview in class.

Student A: You will be the interviewer.
Student B: You will be the candidate.

Topic C

The interview

This is part of the interview between Tim Schneider and the personnel manager, Jack Artner, at NetCom.

Jack Artner: Good afternoon, Mr Schneider. My name is Artner.
Tim Schneider: Nice to meet you, Mr Artner.
...
Jack Artner: Well, do you have any questions?
Tim Schneider: Yes, I'd really like to know some more details about your company ...

a Copy the chart. Then listen to the cassette. Try to remember as many facts as possible concerning the keywords in the chart.

	Tim Schneider
Education and training	?
Reasons for applying	?
Work experience	?
Candidate's strengths	?
Job-related interests	?
Extracurricular activities	?

b Work in groups. Assess the candidate's performance. How well did Tim manage to "sell" himself? Mark your opinion on a scale from 1 (very well) to 5 (badly). Discuss your opinion in the group.

very well	1
well	2
quite well	3
not very well	4
badly	5

"Six thousand a year may not sound much, but look at it this way."

c Work in pairs. Listen to the interview (page 115) again. Try to remember as many questions as possible and write them down. Then ask your partner to answer these questions for him- or herself.

d Role play. Practise interviewing with a partner. Follow the steps in the box below. You might want to look at your CV which you wrote in Unit 7 (page 105).

Student A: Play the role of the interviewer.
Student B: Play the role of the candidate.

Student A	Student B
▪ greeting and small talk	▪ greeting, positive response
▪ reasons for applying	▪ give information about yourself and your company
▪ qualifications and experience	▪ apprenticeship, company training courses, seminars
▪ long- and short-term goals	▪ assistant marketing manager, increasing sales volume
▪ strengths and weaknesses	▪ working under pressure, decision making
▪ closing remarks	▪ express hope for a positive reply, say where you can be reached by phone

Topic D

Job application

Application

Date ③ ______

Phone No. ④ ______

Name	① ______ Last	② ______ First	
Home address	⑤ ______ Street	⑥ ______ City	⑦ ______ Postcode
Position desired	⑧ ______		

	School or College	From To
Education	⑨ ______	⑩ ______
	⑪ ______	⑫ ______
	⑬ ______	⑭ ______

	Employer	From To
Work experience	⑮ ______	⑯ ______
	⑰ ______	⑱ ______

Additional information — Hobbies/Interests ⑲ ______

Other job-relevant activities ⑳ ______

Comments regarding qualifications for employment

㉑ ______

㉒ ______

㉓ ______

a Match the information (A–W) with the numbers (1–23) given on the application form. You will be given an empty application form to fill in.

Example:
⑥ (City) – B. (München)

A. 089/8938062
B. ~~München~~
C. 1990–91
D. Schneider
E. Apprenticeship at C-Base, Düsseldorf
F. Tim
G. Grundschule Unter den Linden
H. Springfield High School, Illinois
I. 80802
J. Marketing assistant
K. 1994 –
L. 12 June, 199...
M. Leopoldstr. 8a
N. Tournament table tennis
O. Good computer skills
P. 1984–90
Q. Wissmann Realschule
R. 1980–84
S. Microware, München
T. Very good knowledge of English
U. Fair working knowledge of French
V. Voluntary work with youth groups
W. 1991–94

b Your teacher will give you an application form. Fill it in with information of your own.

c Work in pairs. Exchange your application form with your partner's. Question your partner on two or three pieces of information you would like to know more about.

d Draft your letter of application based on the information given in the application form. Then read it out to the class.

Useful phrases

A job interview

Interviewer

What do you know about ...?	Was wissen Sie über ...?
Why would you like ...	Warum möchten Sie ...?
What are your reasons for ...?	Weshalb ...?
What are your qualifications?	Was für Qualifikationen haben Sie?
What are your strengths/weaknesses?	Was sind Ihre Stärken/Schwächen?
What has been your most rewarding experience?	Welche Erfahrung war für Sie am lohnendsten?
What have you enjoyed most/least?	Was hat Ihnen am meisten/am wenigsten Spaß gemacht?
What have you learned from ...?	Was haben Sie von/aus ... gelernt?

Candidate

I've been interested in ...	Mich interessiert .../Ich habe Interesse an ...
I've been working with ...	Ich habe mit/bei ... gearbeitet.
I think that ...	Ich denke, dass ...
I believe that ...	Ich glaube, dass ...
I'm convinced that ...	Ich bin überzeugt davon, dass ...
I'd like to know more about ...	Ich würde gerne mehr über ... wissen.
I'm open to new ideas.	Ich bin für neue Ideen aufgeschlossen.
I enjoyed particularly/especially ...	Besonders viel Spaß hat mir ... gemacht.
Least of all ... I enjoyed ...	Am wenigsten Spaß hat mir ... gemacht.

Index

Grammar

Grammatik

1 **Verb forms** Verbformen

	regular	***irregular***
infinitive	work	go
present simple	work/works	go/goes
past simple	worked	went
past participle	worked	gone
-ing-Form	working	going

I wanted to **work**. I must **go**.	Ich wollte arbeiten. Ich muss gehen.
He **goes** to the cinema every week.	Er geht jede Woche ins Kino.
We **went** to the cinema yesterday.	Wir sind gestern ins Kino gegangen.
She's always **worked** hard. They'd **gone** on holiday.	Sie hat immer hart gearbeitet. Sie waren in Urlaub gefahren.
I'm not **working** tomorrow.	Ich arbeite morgen nicht.

2 **Tenses** Zeitformen

	simple		
present	I/we/you/they she/he/it		work works
past	I/she/he/it/ we/you/they		worked
present perfect	I/we/you/they she/he/it	've / have 's / has	worked
past perfect	I/she/he/it/ we/you/they	'd / had	worked

	continuous		
present	I she/he/it we/you/they	'm / am 's / is 're/are	working
past	I/she/he/it we/you/they	was were	working
present perfect	I/we/you/they she/he/it	've / have 's / has	been working
past perfect	I/she/he/it/ we/you/they	'd / had	been working

3 Simple forms and continuous forms
Einfache Formen und Verlaufsformen

- Die Verlaufsform wird aus einer Form von *be* + Verb + *-ing* gebildet.
- Im Gegensatz zu den einfachen Formen verleihen die Verlaufsformen einer Handlung oder einem Ereignis die Eigenschaft der (begrenzten) **Dauer**.

I **work** in Munich. I'**m working** late tonight.	Ich arbeite in München. Heute Abend arbeite ich lange.

4 Short forms Kurzformen

- Im gesprochenen Englisch sind die Kurzformen die üblichen Formen, weil sie neutral sind.

I'm British.	Ich bin Brite/Britin.
◆ Is that your new car? ▲ No, it **isn't**; it'**s** my brother's.	◆ Ist das dein neues Auto? ▲ Nein, es gehört meinem Bruder.

- Wenn im gesprochenen Englisch lange Formen benutzt werden, sind sie meist besonders betont und fügen einer Äußerung zusätzliche Information hinzu (z.B. Widerspruch des Sprechers).

◆ Of course I'm right! ▲ You **are** right in this case, but that doesn't mean you're always right.	◆ Natürlich hab ich Recht! ▲ In diesem Fall hast du Recht, aber das heißt nicht, dass du immer Recht hast.

- Im geschriebenen Englisch werden im Allgemeinen die langen Formen bevorzugt.

5 Important forms of *be* Wichtige Formen von *be*

		bejaht	verneint
present simple	I she/he/it we/you/they	'm / am 's / is 're / are	'm not / am not isn't / 's not / is not aren't / 're not / are not
past simple	I/she/he/it we/you/they	was were	wasn't / was not weren't / were not
present perfect simple	I/we/you/they she/he/it	've / have 's / has been	haven't / 've not / have not hasn't / 's not / has not been
past perfect simple	I/she/he/it/ we/you/they	'd / had been	hadn't / 'd not / had not been
		Frage bejaht	**Frage verneint**
present simple	I she/he/it we/you/they	am I? is she? are we?	aren't I? isn't she? aren't we?
past simple	I/she/he/it we/you/they	was I? were we?	wasn't I? weren't we?
present perfect simple	I/we/you/they she/he/it	have I has she been?	haven't I hasn't she been?
past perfect simple	I/she/he/it/ we/you/they	had I been?	hadn't I been?

Is he in the office today? — Ist er heute im Büro?
He **was** sure he **had been** there before. — Er war sich sicher, dass er schon einmal dort gewesen war.

- *there + be* entspricht dem deutschen „es gibt, es ist/sind, es steht/stehen". *There is/was* wird für die Einzahl benutzt. *There are/were* wird für die Mehrzahl benutzt.

There's a bank in King Street. — Es gibt eine Bank in King Street.
Is there a telephone box near here? — Gibt es hier in der Nähe eine Telefonzelle?
There are a lot of people here tonight. — Es sind heute Abend viele Leute hier.
Weren't there any tickets left? — Gab es keine Karten mehr?

- Formen von *be* werden zur Bildung von Verlaufsformen und Passiv verwendet.

◆ **Are** you doing anything tonight? ◆ Hast du heute Abend etwas vor?
▲ Yes, I'**m** visiting friends. ▲ Ja, ich besuche Freunde.

Our hardware **was** shipped to New York by mistake. Unsere Hardware wurde versehentlich nach New York versandt.

6 Important forms of *have* and *have got*
Wichtige Formen von *have* und *have got*

Have		bejaht	verneint	Frage bejaht	Frage verneint
present simple	I/we/you/they	've / have	haven't / 've not / have not	have I?	haven't I?
	she/he/it	's / has	hasn't / 's not / has not	has she?	hasn't she?
past simple	I/she/he/it we/you/they	'd / had	hadn't / 'd not / had not	had I?	hadn't I?

- Formen von *have* werden zur Bildung von Zeitformen *(present perfect, past perfect)* verwendet.

They **haven't sold** their house yet. Sie haben ihr Haus noch nicht verkauft.

Have you **been** to Munich? Sind Sie schon einmal in München gewesen?

He **had** never **eaten** goulash. Er hatte noch nie Gulasch gegessen.

Have got		bejaht	verneint	Frage bejaht	Frage verneint
present simple	I/we/you/they	've got / have got	haven't got / 've not got / have not got	have I got?	haven't I got?
	she/he/it	's got / has got	hasn't got / 's not got / has not got	has she got?	hasn't she got?
past simple	I/she/he/it we/you/they	'd got / had got	didn't have / did not have	did I have? did she have?	didn't I have? didn't she have?

- *Have got* und *have* haben die gleiche Bedeutung, wenn es um Zugehörigkeit und Beziehungen geht. Im alltäglichen britischen Englisch ist *have got* üblicher. Amerikaner benutzen häufiger *have* ohne *got*.

- Bei *had* (Vergangenheit) wird *got* seltener benutzt. Frage und Verneinung in der Vergangenheit werden gewöhnlich mit *did* gebildet.

I**'ve got** three children.	Ich habe drei Kinder.
She**'s got** relatives in Britain.	Sie hat Verwandte in Großbritannien.
Have you **got** any fruit salad?	Haben Sie Obstsalat?
What type of accommodation **did** Tim **have**?	Was für eine Unterkunft hatte Tim?

7 Important forms of *do* Wichtige Formen von *do*

		bejaht	verneint	Frage bejaht	Frage verneint
present simple	I/we/you/they	do	don't / do not	do you?	don't you?
	she/he/it	does	doesn't / does not	does she?	doesn't she?
past simple	I/she/he/it/ we/you/they	did	didn't / did not	did you?	didn't you?

- Formen von *do* werden zur Bildung von Verneinung und Frage verwendet.

I **don't like** it.	Ich mag das nicht.
Do you **come** here often?	Kommst du öfter hierher?
What time **did** you **get** home last night?	Wann bist du gestern Abend/Nacht nach Hause gekommen?

8 Negative statements Verneinte Aussagesätze

		bejaht		verneint	
present simple	I/we/you/they		work	don't / do not	work
	she/he/it		works	doesn't / does not	work
past simple	I/she/he/it/ we/you/they		worked	didn't / did not	work
present perfect simple	I/we/you/they	've / have	worked	haven't / have not	worked
	she/he/it	's / has	worked	hasn't / has not	worked
past perfect simple	I/she/he/it we/you/they	'd / had	worked	hadn't / had not	worked

- Verneinung im *present* und *past: do + not* + Verb
  Verneinung im *present perfect* und *past perfect: have + not* + Verb

9 Questions Fragebildung

	Aussage			Frage	
present simple	I/we/you/they she/he/it		work works	do you does she	work? work?
past simple	I/she/he/it we/you/they		worked	did she	work?
present perfect simple	I/we/you/they she/he/it	've / have 's / has	worked worked	have you has she	worked? worked?
past perfect simple	I/she/he/it/ we/you/they	'd / had	worked	had she	worked?

- Grundsätzlich gilt:
  Fragebildung **mit** *do* → kein anderes Hilfsverb im Satz
  Fragebildung **ohne** *do* → ein oder mehrere Hilfsverben im Satz

◆ **Do** you work part-time?
▲ Yes, I do. You too?
◆ No, I don't. I've got a full-time job now.

◆ Arbeitest du Teilzeit?
▲ Ja, und du?
◆ Nein, ich habe jetzt eine Ganztagsarbeit.

Has she always worked for Microware? — Hat sie immer schon bei Microware gearbeitet?
Can you bring me the menu, please? — Können Sie mir bitte die Speisekarte bringen?
Have you got lamb chops today? — Gibt es heute Lammkoteletts?

- Die wichtigsten Fragewörter: *who, whose, what, which, where, why, how, when*

Who can you ask for help? — Wen kann man um Hilfe bitten?
What do they like for lunch? — Was möchten sie gern zu Mittag essen?
Which gate should I go to? — Zu welchem Flugsteig sollte ich gehen?
Where does she work? — Wo arbeitet sie?
Why wouldn't you answer my question? — Warum wollten Sie meine Frage nicht beantworten?
How do you get to work? — Wie kommen Sie zur Arbeit?
When do you get up? — Wann stehst du auf?

- Die englischen Fragewörter *who* und *where* lassen sich leicht mit ihren deutschen „falschen Freunden" verwechseln:

Who = Wer
Where = Wo

10 Imperative Aufforderungen

- Diese Form wird verwendet, um Anweisungen, Aufforderungen, Einladungen oder Warnungen auszudrücken.

Turn left/right.	Biegen Sie links/rechts ab.
Go straight ahead!	Gehen Sie geradeaus!
Join our team!	Kommen Sie zu uns!
Don't be afraid!	Hab keine Angst!
Let's go on a cycling holiday!	Lass uns Urlaub mit dem Fahrrad machen!

11 Present simple

Diese Zeitform wird benutzt, um aus der Sicht des Sprechers

- auszudrücken, dass Handlungen/Ereignisse regelmäßig stattfinden.

I **go** to the cinema quite often.	Ich gehe relativ oft ins Kino.

- Fakten auszudrücken.

Wellington **is** the capital of New Zealand.	Wellington ist die Hauptstadt von Neuseeland.
I **don't like** spaghetti.	Ich mag keine Spaghetti.

- über die Zukunft bekannte Tatsachen auszudrücken, insbesondere bei Fahrplänen und feststehenden Terminen.

The train **leaves** at 3 o'clock.	Der Zug fährt um 3 Uhr.

(vgl. auch S. 130, *present simple for talking about the future*)

12 Present continuous

Diese Zeitform wird verwendet, um aus der Sicht des Sprechers

- auszudrücken, dass Handlungen/Ereignisse sich auf den Moment des Sprechens beziehen.

Somebody**'s stealing** your car.	Da stiehlt jemand Ihr Auto.

- auszudrücken, dass Handlungen, Zustände usw. nur vorübergehend sind.

I usually cycle to work but **I'm going** by bus at the moment because it's so cold.	Normalerweise fahre ich mit dem Rad zur Arbeit, aber zur Zeit fahre ich mit dem Bus, weil es so kalt ist.
Aren't you **feeling** very well?	Fühlst du dich nicht wohl?

- Verabredungen, Pläne und Absichten für die Zukunft auszudrücken.

I'm having dinner with Tim on Thursday.	Am Donnerstag bin ich mit Tim zum Abendessen verabredet.
Where **are** you **going** on holiday next year?	Wohin fährst du nächstes Jahr in Urlaub?

(vgl. auch S. 130, *present continuous for talking about the future*)

13 Past simple

- Diese Zeitform wird häufig verwendet, wenn es sich aus der Sicht des Sprechers um punktuelle Handlungen/Ereignisse handelt, die vor dem Moment des Sprechens abgeschlossen sind.

My grandfather **died** before I **was born**.	Mein Großvater starb noch vor meiner Geburt.
Did you **enjoy** your holiday?	War es schön im Urlaub?

- Zeitangaben mit *last (last week, year, etc.)* und *ago (two seconds ago, two centuries ago, etc.)* verlangen in der Regel *past tense.*

Last May we **flew** to Boston.	Wir sind letzten Mai nach Boston geflogen.
During my last holiday I **slept** in a tent.	Während meines letzten Urlaubs habe ich im Zelt geschlafen.
We **spent** a weekend in Zurich five years ago.	Vor fünf Jahren haben wir ein Wochenende in Zürich verbracht.

14 Past continuous

Diese Zeitform wird verwendet, um

- vergangene Handlungen/Ereignisse von begrenzter Dauer auszudrücken.

I **was waiting** for you in front of the hotel, but you didn't come.	Ich habe vor dem Hotel auf dich gewartet, aber du bist nicht gekommen.

- ein Ereignis auszudrücken, das schon im Gange war, als eine weitere Handlung einsetzte.

When we left the house, the sun **was shining**.	Als wir aus dem Haus kamen, schien die Sonne.

15 Present perfect simple

Diese Zeitform wird häufig verwendet, wenn

- der Sprecher auf Handlungen/Ereignisse zurückschaut und deren Auswirkungen auf die Gegenwart oder Zukunft in den Mittelpunkt stellt.

I **haven't done** it yet.	Ich habe es noch nicht gemacht. (Die Arbeit liegt immer noch unerledigt da.)
The children **have made** a terrible mess.	Die Kinder haben eine furchtbare Schweinerei veranstaltet (und ich werde jetzt aufräumen müssen).

- Handlungen/Ereignisse in der Vergangenheit angefangen haben und noch andauern.

He**'s been** unemployed for two years. *vgl.:*	Er ist seit zwei Jahren arbeitslos (und ist es immer noch).
He was unemployed for two years.	Er war zwei Jahre arbeitslos (und hat jetzt wieder Arbeit).

- Fragen sich auf einen Zeitraum bis hin zum Moment des Sprechens beziehen.

Have you ever **been** to Texas?	Waren Sie schon mal in Texas?
vgl.:	
Did you see the Alamo when you were in Texas?	Haben Sie das Alamo gesehen, als Sie in Texas waren?

16 Present perfect continuous

- Diese Zeitform wird verwendet, wenn der Sprecher auf Handlungen/Ereignisse zurückschaut und zusätzlich (begrenzte) Dauer betonen will.

◆ How long **have** you **been living** in Germany?	◆ Wie lange lebst du schon in Deutschland?
▲ I**'ve been living** here for 15 years.	▲ Ich lebe seit 15 Jahren hier.
◆ Why are you crying?	◆ Warum weinst du?
▲ I**'ve been chopping** onions for the last half hour.	▲ Weil ich seit einer halben Stunde dabei bin, Zwiebeln klein zu hacken.
vgl.:	
◆ Why are you crying?	◆ Warum weinst du?
▲ I've just cut my finger with the kitchen knife.	▲ Ich habe mich gerade mit dem Küchenmesser in den Finger geschnitten.

17 Past perfect simple

- Diese Zeitform wird verwendet, wenn der Sprecher von einem Punkt in der Vergangenheit auf einen noch früheren Zeitpunkt zurückschaut.

When I got home I found that the children **had made** a terrible mess.	Als ich nach Hause kam, entdeckte ich, dass die Kinder eine furchtbare Schweinerei veranstaltet hatten.
He **had been** unemployed for two years when the accident happened.	Er war schon zwei Jahre arbeitslos, als der Unfall passierte.

18 Past perfect continuous

- Diese Zeitform wird verwendet, wenn der Sprecher von einem Punkt in der Vergangenheit auf einen noch früheren Zeitpunkt zurückschaut und zusätzlich die (begrenzte) Dauer einer Handlung betonen will.

When I got home he was crying because he**'d been chopping** onions.	Als ich nach Hause kam, weinte er, weil er Zwiebeln klein gehackt hatte.

19 Talking about the future Zukunft ausdrücken

Im Englischen gibt es mehrere Möglichkeiten, über die Zukunft zu sprechen.

- *be + going to + infinitive*
  Diese Form wird häufig verwendet, wenn
  – es für den Sprecher deutliche Hinweise gibt, dass etwas geschehen wird.

I'm going to be sick.	Ich muss mich gleich übergeben.
It**'s going to snow** any time now.	Es wird jeden Moment schneien.

  – es um eine langfristige oder überlegte Entscheidung geht.

I'm going to fly to Brussels on Monday.	Ich werde am Montag nach Brüssel fliegen.

- *will/'ll*
  Diese Form wird häufig verwendet, um über die Zukunft bekannte Tatsachen oder Vorhersagen auszudrücken.

We**'ll be** on holiday next week.	Wir werden nächste Woche im Urlaub sein.
She **won't be** in the office this afternoon.	Sie wird heute Nachmittag nicht im Büro sein.
Do you think I**'ll get** the job?	Meinst du, dass ich die Stelle bekommen werde?
It**'ll** probably **rain** tomorrow.	Morgen wird es wahrscheinlich regnen.

- *present continuous*
  Diese Form wird häufig verwendet, um Verabredungen, Pläne und Absichten für die Zukunft auszudrücken.

I'm visiting the fair in Frankfurt on Wednesday.	Am Mittwoch bin ich auf der Messe in Frankfurt.
What time **is** Tim **attending** the staff meeting on Friday?	Wann geht Tim am Freitag zur Mitarbeiterbesprechung?

- *present simple*
  Diese Form wird verwendet, um über die Zukunft bekannte Tatsachen auszudrücken, insbesondere bei Fahrplänen und feststehenden Terminen.

The train **leaves** at 3 o'clock.	Der Zug fährt um 3 Uhr.

20 Passive forms Passivformen

present	I she/he/it we/you/they		am is are	needed
past	I/she/he/it we/you/they		was were	needed
present perfect	I/we/you/they she/he/it	have has	been	needed
past perfect	I/she/he/it we/you/they	had	been	needed

- Die Passivformen werden aus einer Form von *be* + *past participle* des Verbs gebildet.
- Die Passivformen werden verwendet, wenn aus der Sicht des Sprechers der Handelnde unbekannt oder weniger interessant ist als die Handlung selbst.

English **is spoken** all over the world.	Englisch wird auf der ganzen Welt gesprochen.
A new telecommunications system **has been developed**.	Ein neues Telekommunikationssystem ist entwickelt worden.

- Der Handelnde wird nur erwähnt, wenn es aus der Sicht des Sprechers um eine wichtige Zusatzinformation geht.

English **is spoken by** millions of people.	Englisch wird von Millionen von Menschen gesprochen.
A new telecommunications system **was developed by** Electro Sul.	Ein neues Telekommunikationssystem wurde von Electro Sul entwickelt.

21 Modal verbs Modale Hilfsverben

Diese Verben weisen einige Besonderheiten auf:

– Sie haben für alle Personen (*I, she, he, it, we,* etc.) die gleiche Form, d.h. sie haben in der 3. Person Singular kein *-s*.
– Sie können keine *-ing*-Form bilden.
– Einige kommen nur in der Zeitform *present*, einige nur im *past* vor.
– Sie bilden Frage und Verneinung ohne *do*.

Zu den modalen Hilfsverben gehören:

will/would	ought to	can/could	must	have (got) to
shall/should	had better	may/might	need (not)	used to

a *Will*

bejaht	verneint
'll will	won't will not

- Absicht/Versprechen

I'll book you on the 8.05 flight from Munich. — Ich buche für Sie den Flug um 8.05 Uhr von München.
We'll bring something to eat. — Wir bringen etwas zu essen mit.
Will you be in on Sunday? — Seid ihr am Sonntag zu Hause?
I won't do it again. — Ich tu's nicht wieder.

- spontane Entscheidung

I'll have the roast beef. — Ich nehme das Roastbeef.
I've got a headache – I think I'll take an aspirin. — Ich habe Kopfschmerzen, ich nehme mal ein Aspirin.

- Bitte

Will you help me finish this? — Hilfst du mir, das hier fertig zu machen?

- über die Zukunft bekannte Fakten/Vorhersagen

We'll be at the fair in Boston next week. — Wir werden nächste Woche auf der Messe in Boston sein.
It'll probably rain tomorrow. — Morgen wird es wahrscheinlich regnen.

- in Bedingungssätzen

Muster:	*if*-Satz → *present* Hauptsatz → *'ll/will*

If you start now, you'll have plenty of time. — Wenn du jetzt losfährst, wirst du noch viel Zeit haben.

b *Would*

bejaht	verneint
'd would	wouldn't would not

- Angebot/Einladung

◆ Would you like a cup of coffee? ▲ Yes, I'd love a cup.	◆ Möchten Sie eine Tasse Kaffee? ▲ Ja, gerne.
Would you like to come for a meal on Wednesday?	Möchten Sie am Mittwoch zum Essen kommen?

- Wünsche

I'd like a map of London.	Ich hätte gern einen Stadtplan von London.

- Bitte

Would you hold this for a moment, please?	Würdest du das bitte einen Moment halten?

- Ratschlag

◆ What would you do? ▲ If I were you, I'd go and see the exhibitions in the Pinakothek.	◆ Was würdest du machen? ▲ An deiner Stelle würde ich mir die Ausstellungen in der Pinakothek ansehen.

- in Bedingungssätzen

Muster:	*if*-Satz → *past* Hauptsatz → *would*	*if*-Satz → *past perfect* Hauptsatz → *would have*

I wouldn't drink so much if I were you.	An deiner Stelle würde ich nicht so viel trinken.
If I missed my flight, I'd try to get the next one.	Wenn ich meinen Flug verpassen würde, würde ich versuchen den nächsten zu bekommen.
If I had missed my flight, I would have tried to get the next one.	Wenn ich meinen Flug verpasst hätte, hätte ich versucht den nächsten zu bekommen.
You'd have loved the food!	Das Essen hätte dir geschmeckt! (wenn du da gewesen wärst)

c *Shall*

bejaht	**verneint**
shall	(shan't) (shall not)

- Vorschlag

Shall we take the direct flight? Shall I give her a message? Shall we buy her flowers?	Wollen wir den Direktflug nehmen? Soll ich ihr etwas ausrichten? Sollen wir ihr Blumen kaufen?

d *Should*

bejaht	verneint
should	shouldn't should not

- Ratschlag

You should eat more fruit. — Du solltest mehr Obst essen.
You shouldn't smoke so much. — Du solltest nicht so viel rauchen.
You shouldn't tell other people what to do. — Du solltest anderen Leuten nicht sagen, was sie machen sollen.
Shouldn't you have come earlier? — Hättest du nicht früher kommen sollen?

e *Ought to*

bejaht	verneint
ought to	ought not to

- (moralische) Verpflichtung

We ought to write and thank them. — Wir sollten ihnen eigentlich schreiben und uns bedanken.

People ought not to dump rubbish in the woods. — Die Leute sollten ihren Müll nicht im Wald abladen.

f *Had better*

bejaht	verneint
'd better had better	'd better not had better not

- Ratschlag/Warnung

I think you'd better go. — Ich glaube, du solltest jetzt gehen.
You'd better talk to him about the problem. — Du solltest eigentlich mit ihm über das Problem sprechen.
Hadn't we better meet well in advance? — Sollten wir uns nicht rechtzeitig vorher treffen?

g *Can*

bejaht	verneint
can	can't cannot

- Fähigkeit/Möglichkeit

I can swim. I can't come on Friday.	Ich kann schwimmen. Ich kann am Freitag nicht kommen.
◆ Can you type?	◆ Kannst du Schreibmaschine schreiben?
▲ No, I can't I'm afraid.	▲ Nein, leider nicht.

- Erlaubnis/Verbot

You can smoke here. You can't park here.	Sie können hier rauchen. Sie können hier nicht parken.

- Bitte/Angebot

Can I use your phone?	Kann ich Ihr Telefon benutzen?
Can I speak to Mr Hill, please?	Kann ich bitte Herrn Hill sprechen?
You can use it for setting up a new filing system.	Sie können damit ein neues Ablagesystem einrichten.

h *Could*

bejaht	verneint
could	couldn't could not

- Fähigkeit/Möglichkeit

When I was young I could dance all night.	Als ich jung war, konnte ich die ganze Nacht durchtanzen.
I could come on Friday if necessary.	Falls nötig, könnte ich am Freitag kommen.
It couldn't have been better!	Das hätte nicht besser sein können!

- höfliche Bitte/Vorschlag

Could you type this letter, please?	Könnten Sie bitte diesen Brief schreiben?
Could you repeat that, please?	Könnten Sie das bitte wiederholen?

- Annahme

It could be a device for video-conferencing. | Es könnte (vielleicht) ein Gerät für Videokonferenzen sein.

i *May*

bejaht	verneint
may	may not

- Wahrscheinlichkeit

We may see you next week. | Vielleicht sehen wir Sie nächste Woche.
They may not have heard the news. | Vielleicht haben sie die Neuigkeit noch nicht gehört.

- höfliche Bitte/Erlaubnis

May I open the window? | Darf ich vielleicht das Fenster aufmachen?

May I introduce you to Ms Beyer? | Darf ich Ihnen Frau Beyer vorstellen?

j *Might*

bejaht	verneint
might	mightn't might not

- Wahrscheinlichkeit (weniger sicher als *may*)

We might be a little bit late. | Es könnte sein, dass wir ein bisschen später kommen.

It might be an old-fashioned typewriter. | Es könnte eine alte Schreibmaschine sein.

k *Must*

bejaht	verneint
must	mustn't must not

- Notwendigkeit (inneres Bedürfnis)

I must get something to drink. | Ich muss mir etwas zu trinken holen.

- Verbot

Passengers must not carry dangerous articles in their luggage. — Passagiere dürfen keine gefährlichen Gegenstände in ihrem Gepäck mitführen.

Merke: „du musst nicht“ = *you needn't/don't need to*

- logische Schlussfolgerung

That must be the Regent Hotel. — Das muss das Regent Hotel sein.

l *Need (not)*

bejaht	**verneint**
(need)	needn't need not

- fehlende Notwendigkeit (Gegenteil von *must*)

We needn't go yet. — Wir müssen noch nicht weg.
We needn't be there till 8 o'clock. — Wir brauchen nicht vor acht da zu sein.

m *Have (got) to*

	present		***past***	
	bejaht	**verneint**	**bejaht**	**verneint**
I/we/you/they she/he/it	've /have 's /has got to	haven't hasn't got to	had to	didn't have to
I/we/you/they she/he/it	have to has to	don't / do not have to doesn't / does not have to		did not have to

- äußere Notwendigkeit

In this job you have to know English. — In diesem Beruf muss man Englisch können.
Is it free or have we got to pay? — Ist es umsonst oder müssen wir zahlen?
Doesn't he have to do shiftwork now? — Muss er jetzt nicht Schicht arbeiten?

We didn't have to wait long.	Wir mussten nicht lange warten.
We'll have to report it to the police.	Das werden wir der Polizei melden müssen.
Do I have to change trains?	Muss ich umsteigen?
You have to look out for the shuttle service which leaves in front of the hotel.	Sie müssen auf den Pendelbus achten, der vor dem Hotel abfährt.

n *Used to*

bejaht	**verneint**
used to	didn't used to

- frühere Gewohnheiten/Zustände

We used to come here quite often. (we don't now)	Früher waren wir oft hier. (jetzt nicht mehr)
There didn't used to be a factory here.	Früher war hier keine Fabrik.
I used to go dancing a lot when I was younger.	Früher, als ich noch jünger war, ging ich oft zum Tanzen.

22 Noun plurals Mehrzahl von Nomen

Einzahl	**Mehrzahl**	**regelmäßig**
arm brother	arm**s** brother**s**	*+ -s*
bu**s** dre**ss** chur**ch** bo**x**	bus**es** dress**es** church**es** box**es**	*+ -es*
lad**y** secretar**y**	lad**ies** secretar**ies**	*-y → -ies*
tomat**o** potat**o**	tomat**oes** potat**oes**	*-o → -oes**
hal**f** shel**f**	hal**ves** shel**ves**	*-f → -ves**
child foot man woman	children feet men women	unregelmäßig*

* Es handelt sich hier um häufige Beispiele.

23 Countable and uncountable nouns Zählbare und nichtzählbare Nomen

- zählbar:

  one child → **two** children / **a** country → **several** countries /
  one man → **many** men

Merke: *how many children, countries, men ...?*

- werden meistens nicht gezählt:

  Stoffe: *bread, butter, coffee, earth*
  Eigenschaften: *humour, intelligence, pride*
  abstrakte Begriffe: *fun, health, politics, weather*

  Nichtzählbare Nomen haben keine Mehrzahl und können nicht mit *a(n)* verwendet werden.

Merke: *how much bread, butter ...?*

- Manche Wörter können je nach Bedeutung zählbar oder nichtzählbar sein:

  rubber = Gummi / *a rubber* = ein Radiergummi
  iron = Eisen / *an iron* = ein Bügeleisen
  coffee = Kaffee / *a coffee* = eine Tasse Kaffee
  cheese = Käse / *230 different cheeses* = 230 Käsesorten

- Abweichend vom Deutschen sind einige Wörter im Englischen nichtzählbar, z.B.: *advice, furniture, information, news, money*

Merke: **eine** Information/Nachricht = *a(n) bit/item/piece of information/ news*

24 *'s*-genitive *'s*-Genitiv

- Diese Form wird bei Menschen und Tieren verwendet, um Besitz oder Zugehörigkeit auszudrücken:

  Jenn**y's** computer / St Mary**'s** church / Ms Beyer**'s** extension / the dog**'s** bone

Merke: at the butcher's (= at the butcher's shop) / at the doctor's at Pat's (= bei Pat)

- In der Mehrzahl bei schon vorhandenem *s:*

  rabbit**s'** noses (Einzahl: a rabbit**'s** nose)
  spider**s'** webs (Einzahl: a spider**'s** web)

- Statt *'s*-Genitiv wird meist *of* benutzt
  - wenn es nicht um Menschen/Tiere geht
  - bei Mengenangaben

  the roof of the house / the taste of coffee / a kilo of tomatoes

25 Use of the article in English and German
Gebrauch des Artikels im Englischen und Deutschen

- unbestimmter Artikel: *an* vor *a/e/i/o/u* (an electrician, an orange) und vor stummem *h* (an hour)
  a vor allen anderen Buchstaben (a book, a man)
- bestimmter Artikel: *the* (the electrician/the hour [ðɪ] /the book/the man [ðə])
- Der Gebrauch des Artikels ist in beiden Sprachen weitgehend ähnlich. Folgende Unterschiede sollte man sich aber merken:

She's **a** sales rep / **an** engineer.	Sie ist Vertreterin / Ingenieurin.
twice **a** week / once **a** year	zweimal **die** Woche / einmal **im** Jahr
It costs 60p **a** pound.	Es kostet 60p **das** Pfund.
play **the** piano/**the** flute	Klavier/Flöte spielen
I live in King Street.	Ich wohne in **der** King Street.
by bike / by bus	mit **dem** Rad / mit **dem** Bus

26 Personal, possessive and reflexive pronouns
Personal-, Possessiv- und Reflexivpronomen

Personalpronomen		**Possessivpronomen**		**Reflexivpronomen**
(1)	(2)	(3)	(4)	(5)
I	me	my	mine	myself
she	her	her	hers	herself
he	him	his	his	himself
it	it	its		itself
we	us	our	ours	ourselves
you	you	your	yours	yourself*/yourselves**
they	them	their	theirs	themselves

* Einzahl ** Mehrzahl

She[1] saw **me**[2] coming.	Sie sah mich kommen.
I[1] wanted to give **him**[2] **his**[3] book back.	Ich wollte ihm sein Buch zurückgeben.
He[1] thought **it**[1] was **mine**[4] but actually **it**[1] belongs to a friend of **ours**[4], so I'm afraid **you**[1] can't have **it**[2].	Er hat gedacht, es sei meins, aber in Wirklichkeit gehört es einem Freund von uns, deshalb kannst du es leider nicht haben.

Their[3] son had an accident and cut **himself**[5] badly.	Ihr Sohn hatte einen Unfall und hat sich eine ziemlich schlimme Schnittverletzung zugezogen.

27 Demonstrative pronouns (*this – that, these – those)*
Demonstrativpronomen

- *this/these:* nahe aus der Sicht des Sprechers
  that/these: nicht so nahe aus der Sicht des Sprechers

◆ Have you got a pullover like this but in blue?	◆ Haben Sie so einen Pullover in Blau?
▲ Have a look at those over there, madam.	▲ Schauen Sie sich die da drüben an.
These are the in-trays. Those are the out-trays.	Dies hier ist die Posteingangsablage. Dort drüben ist die Postausgangsablage.
This is Mary O'Neill speaking.	Hier spricht Mary O'Neill.
Who was that on the phone just now?	Wer war das gerade am Telefon?

28 Relative pronouns (*who, which, that)* Relativpronomen

- *who* bezieht sich auf Personen, *which* auf Sachen;
  that kann sich auf beides beziehen.

I like teachers who/that prepare their lessons.	Ich mag Lehrer/innen, die ihre Stunden vorbereiten.
I don't like films which/that show a lot of violence.	Ich mag keine Filme, in denen viel Gewalt gezeigt wird.

- *who/which/that* als Objekt des Relativsatzes fallen oft weg.

What's the name of that American (who/that) you used to work with?	Wie heißt der Amerikaner, mit dem du früher zusammengearbeitet hast?
What's the name of the company (which/that) you used to work for?	Wie heißt die Firma, bei der Sie früher gearbeitet haben?

- Im Gegensatz zum Deutschen werden Relativsätze im Englischen in den meisten Fällen nicht durch Kommas abgetrennt.

29 *One(s)*

- *one(s)* wird verwendet, um eine Wiederholung eines vorher genannten oder bekannten Nomens zu vermeiden.

◆ Would you like **a cup of coffee**?	◆ Möchten Sie eine Tasse Kaffee?
▲ Thanks, I'd love **one**.	▲ Ja, gerne.

These **disks** are too expensive. Have you got any cheaper **ones**?	Diese Disketten sind zu teuer. Haben Sie billigere?

30 *Some and any*

- *Some* und *any* entsprechen dem deutschen *etwas, einige*. Im Deutschen verzichtet man häufig auf ein solches Begleitwort.

We need **some** sugar.	Wir brauchen (etwas) Zucker.
We haven't got **any** tea.	Wir haben keinen Tee.

- Bei *some* hat der Sprecher einen Teil aus einer größeren Menge im Auge. Das Gleiche gilt für *somebody, someone, something, somewhere.*

There must be **someone** who can help us.	Es muss doch jemanden geben, der uns helfen kann.
There's **something** I'd like to discuss with you.	Ich möchte da gern etwas mit Ihnen besprechen.

- Bei *any* hat der Sprecher die Vorstellung „alles oder nichts". Das Gleiche gilt für *anybody, anyone, anything, anywhere.*

Anyone can do that – it's easy!	Das kann doch jeder, so einfach ist das!
I'll do **anything** to help her.	Ich tue alles, um ihr zu helfen.

31 Comparison of adjectives Adjektive: Steigerung und Vergleich

- Für die Steigerung gilt im Allgemeinen diese Regel:

einsilbig	long	long**er**	long**est**
einsilbig mit *-y*	happ**y**	happ**ier**	happ**iest**
2 oder mehr Silben	expensive interesting	**more** expensive **more** interesting	**most** expensive **most** interesting

- Unregelmäßig:

good bad	better worse	best worst

- Vergleiche mit *than:*

Letters are normally **longer than** telexes.	Briefe sind normalerweise länger als Fernschreiben.
The train is **more expensive than** the bus.	Die Bahn ist teurer als der Bus.

- Vergleiche mit *as ... as:*

Telexes are normally not **as long as** letters.	Fernschreiben sind normalerweise nicht so lang wie Briefe.
Charter flights are not **as expensive as** ordinary flights.	Charterflüge sind nicht so teuer wie Linienflüge.

32 Formation of adverbs Adverbien: Bildung

	adjective	adverb
regelmäßig	bad careful slow	bad**ly** careful**ly** slow**ly**
unregelmäßig	good better early fast hard	well better early fast hard

I got **bad marks** in the exam.	Ich habe eine schlechte Note in der Prüfung bekommen.
I **did badly** in the exam.	Ich habe schlecht abgeschnitten bei der Prüfung.
Her French is very **good**.	Ihr Französisch ist sehr gut.
She **speaks** French very **well**.	Sie spricht gut Französisch.

33 Comparison of adverbs Adverbien: Vergleiche

- Vergleiche mit *than:*

He walks even **more slowly than** me.	Er läuft noch langsamer als ich.
The driver was **less badly** hurt **than** the passengers.	Der Fahrer wurde weniger schwer verletzt als die Mitfahrer.

- Vergleiche mit *as ... as:*

He did not do **as well as** he expected in the exam.	Er schnitt bei der Prüfung nicht so gut ab, wie er erwartet hatte.
Men do not drive **as carefully as** women.	Männer fahren nicht so vorsichtig wie Frauen.

34 **Frequency adverbs: position** Häufigkeitsadverbien: Stellung

- In Aussagesätzen stehen die weniger präzisen Häufigkeitsadverbien (*seldom*, *quite often*, *hardly ever* usw.) vor einem normalen Verb bzw. nach einem besonderen Verb (*be*, *can* usw.).

I	never occasionally quite often sometimes hardly ever	send a fax.

Ich schicke	nie gelegentlich ziemlich oft sehr selten manchmal	ein Fax.

- Präzisere Beschreibungen der Häufigkeit (every day/Tuesday, twice a week usw.) stehen am Ende des Satzes.

I send a fax	every day. twice a week. once a day. now and again.

Ich schicke	jeden Tag zweimal pro Woche einmal am Tag hin und wieder	ein Fax.

35 **Prepositions** Verhältniswörter

Die meisten englischen Präpositionen bestehen aus einem Wort (z.B. *in*, *on*, *to*, *from*). Es gibt aber auch Präpositionen, die aus zwei oder mehreren Wörtern bestehen (z.B. *next to*, *in front of*, *out of*). Für den Gebrauch von Präpositionen gibt es keine allgemein gültigen Regeln.

The telephone is **on** Tim's desk.	Das Telefon steht auf Tims Schreibtisch.
The filing cabinet is **next to** the photocopier.	Der Aktenschrank steht neben dem Fotokopierer.
The wastepaper basket is **under** Tim's desk.	Der Papierkorb steht unter Tims Schreibtisch.
The stapler is **by** the hole punch.	Die Heftmaschine steht neben dem Locher.

36 **Spelling notes** Anmerkungen zur Rechtschreibung

- Mitlaut + *-y* → *i*

hap**py** t**ry**	→ happier/happiest/happily/happiness → trial/tried

- Mitlaut + *-y* + *-s* → *ie*

ba**by** myste**ry** t**ry**	→ babies → mysteries → tries

- Mitlaut + *-y* + *-ing:* keine Änderung

c**ry** t**ry**	→ crying → trying

- *-ie* + *-ing* → *-y*

d**ie** l**ie**	→ dying → lying

- Mitlaut + stummes *-e* + Selbstlaut → *-e* entfällt (z.B. bei *-ed, -ing*)

deci**de** lo**ve** smi**le**	→ decided, deciding → loved, lover, loving → smiled, smiling

- Bei Ableitungen mit den folgenden Endungen wird der Mitlaut verdoppelt, wenn der vorangehende Selbstlaut mit **einem** Buchstaben geschrieben wird. Zu diesen Endungen gehören: *-ed, -en, -er, -est, -ing, -ish, -y.*

fi**t** ho**t** ro**t** ru**n** sho**p** begi**n** trave**l**	→ fitter/fittest/fitted/fitting → hotter/hottest/hottish → rotted/rotten/rotting → runner/running/runny → shopped/shopper/shopping → beginner/beginning → travelled/travelling

Merke:	keine Verdoppelung im amerikanischen Englisch! travel → traveler, traveled, traveling

37 Numerals Zahlwörter

a Cardinal numbers (Grundzahlen)

0	nought, zero, oh	6	six	12	twelve
1	one	7	seven	13	thirteen
2	two	8	eight	14	fourteen
3	three	9	nine	15	fifteen
4	four	10	ten	16	sixteen
5	five	11	eleven	17	seventeen

18	eighteen	40	forty	90	ninety
19	nineteen	41	forty-one	91	ninety-one
20	twenty	50	fifty	100	a (*or* one) hundred
21	twenty-one	51	fifty-one	101	a (*or* one) hundred and one
22	twenty-two	60	sixty	102	a (*or* one) hundred and two
23	twenty-three	61	sixty-one	110	a (*or* one) hundred and ten
30	thirty	70	seventy	200	two hundred
31	thirty-one	71	seventy-one	300	three hundred
32	thirty-two	80	eighty	451	four hundred and fifty-one
33	thirty-three	81	eighty-one		

1 000	a (*or* one) thousand	1 000 000	a (*or* one) million
2 000	two thousand	2 000 000	two million
10 000	ten thousand	1 000 000 000	a (*or* one) billion
		1 000 000 000 000	a (*or* one) trillion

b Ordinal numbers (Ordnungszahlen)

1st	first	22nd	twenty-second
2nd	second	23rd	twenty-third
3rd	third	30th	thirtieth
4th	fourth	31st	thirty-first
5th	fifth	40th	fortieth
6th	sixth	41st	forty-first
7th	seventh	50th	fiftieth
8th	eighth	51st	fifty-first
9th	ninth	60th	sixtieth
10th	tenth	61st	sixty-first
11th	eleventh	70th	seventieth
12th	twelfth	71st	seventy-first
13th	thirteenth	80th	eightieth
14th	fourteenth	81st	eighty-first
15th	fifteenth	90th	ninetieth
16th	sixteenth	100th	(one) hundredth
17th	seventeenth	101st	hundred and first
18th	eighteenth	200th	two hundredth
19th	nineteenth	300th	three hundredth
20th	twentieth	451st	four hundred and fifty-first
21st	twenty-first	1 000th	(one) thousandth

38 **Time of day** Die Uhrzeit

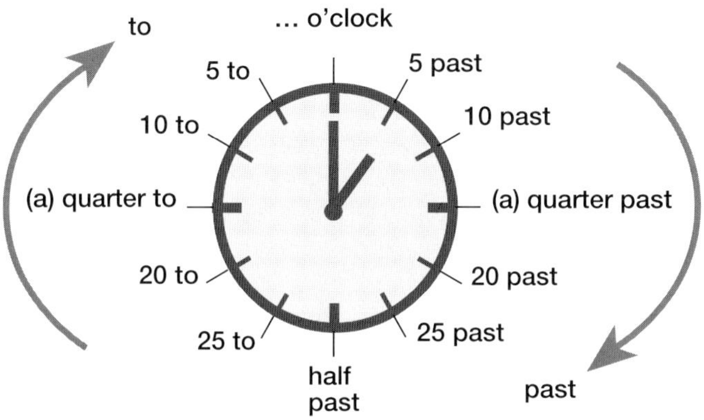

- Im Englischen ist die 24-Stunden-Zählung weniger üblich. Man zählt normalerweise die Stunden bis 12 und beginnt dann wieder von vorne.

  Ausnahme: Der Reiseverkehr. Hier wird die 24-Stunden-Zählung (*24-hour clock*) verwendet.

- Um Verwechselungen zu vermeiden, werden die Stunden von Mitternacht bis Mittag durch *a.m.* (lat. *ante meridiem* = vor Mittag) und die Stunden von Mittag bis Mitternacht mit *p.m.* (lat. *post meridiem* = nach Mittag) gekennzeichnet.

- Im amerikanischen Gebrauch ist neben *past* bzw. *to* auch *after* bzw. *of* geläufig:

  4.10 *ten after four*
  9.45 *(a) quarter of ten*

Listening comprehension texts

Hörverständnistexte

Unit 1

Topic A/b

Patricia Newman: Good morning, Tim. Nice to see you again. How are you?
Tim Schneider: Oh, I'm fine. Thank you.
Patricia Newman: I would like to show you around the marketing department this morning and introduce you to your co-workers.
Tim Schneider: Yes, that would be nice.
Patricia Newman: Of course, we work closely with the sales and advertising departments. Each department has its own small area. I won't introduce you to anyone there today, though. It might be too much for the first day.
Tim Schneider: Okay, that's fine.
Patricia Newman: Mr Williams, the marketing manager isn't in today. You can meet him tomorrow, perhaps.
Tim Schneider: Yes, all right.
Patricia Newman: May I introduce you to Ms Beyer, our secretary. Ms Beyer works for Mr Williams and myself.
Martha, this is Tim Schneider, the new marketing assistant.
Martha Beyer: Hello, Tim. How do you do?
Tim Schneider: How do you do?
Patricia Newman: Good morning, Jenny. I'd like you to meet Tim Schneider. He's the new marketing assistant. He'll be working with Miriam.
Jenny Rose: Hello, Tim. Nice to meet you.
Patricia Newman: We have two secretaries for the sales, advertising and marketing departments. Jenny is one of them and she works with Monika Kühl.
Tim Schneider: Nice to meet you too, Ms Rose.
Jenny Rose: Oh, please call me Jenny.
Tim Schneider: Okay, Jenny.
Patricia Newman: Is Miriam in her office? I thought she could help Tim get settled in this morning.
Jenny Rose: She's just gone to see Anne Miller for a moment. Tim, would you like a cup of coffee until Miriam gets back?
Tim Schneider: Yes, thanks. I'd love one.
Patricia Newman: Okay, great. Tim, Jenny can introduce you to Miriam. She's our other marketing assistant. She can help you with any questions. But don't hesitate to call me if I can help you with anything.
Tim Schneider: Thank you and thank you for showing me around, Ms Newman.
Patricia Newman: Oh, you're very welcome. Goodbye for now.
Tim Schneider: Goodbye.

Topic D/a

1. Take the lift up to the second floor. Turn left and go along to the end of the corridor. Turn right and the conference room is straight ahead at the end of the corridor.
2. Go out of the office and turn right. Go down to the end of the corridor and turn right again. Go down the corridor and the stairs are at the end of the corridor on the left hand side. Go down to the ground floor. Turn left and the canteen is in front of you.
3. Go out of the office and turn left. Take the lift down to the ground floor. Turn left and go straight along to the end of the corridor. Turn right and the post room is the first door on the right.

Unit 2

Topic B/a

Susan Boyd: Microware. Guten Morgen.
Mr Lopez: Good morning, this is Mr Lopez from Electro Sul, Brazil. I'd like to talk to Mr Schneider.
Susan Boyd: Just a moment, Sir. I'll put you through. What was the name, please?
Mr Lopez: Lopez, Carlos Lopez.
Susan Boyd: Could you spell that, please?
Mr Lopez: Yes, that's L.O.P.E.Z.
Susan Boyd: Thank you. Hold the line, please. Oh, I'm sorry, Mr Lopez, but Mr Schneider is not in his office. Would you like to leave a message?
Mr Lopez: Yes, could you please tell him that I called and that I'll try again this afternoon.
Susan Boyd: Certainly, and you can dial directly. His extension number is 803.
Mr Lopez: Thank you, goodbye.

Topic B/e

First call:

Janice: 771 54 20.
Robert: Is that you, Janice?
Janice: Yes, speaking.
Robert: This is Robert. I'm calling from Glasgow.
Janice: Oh, hello, Robert ...

Second call:

Frank Whittle: Frank Whittle speaking.
Sven Erikson: Hello, Mr Whittle this is Sven Erikson from Stockholm. I've just arrived here in London and I'd like to meet you to discuss our new project.
Frank Whittle: Certainly, Mr. Erikson. Let me see ...

Third call:

Receptionist: Inbit. Good afternoon.
Jean Pasquier: Jean Pasquier speaking. Could you please connect me with Ms Grime?
Receptionist: Just a moment, please. What was the name?
Jean Pasquier: Pasquier, P.A.S.Q.U.I.E.R, Jean Pasquier from Paris.

Fourth call:

Sheila Winter: Hello.
Nicos: Is that 665 82 31?
Sheila Winter: Yes, Sheila Winter speaking.
Nicos: Hi, Sheila. It's Nicos. I'm calling from the airport. I'm going on holiday to Greece for three weeks. I just wanted to say goodbye to you.
Sheila Winter: Oh Nicos, that's really nice. I wish you ...

Topic C/a

Tim Schneider: Schneider speaking.
Carlos Lopez: Hello, Mr Schneider. This is Carlos Lopez from Electro Sul, Brazil. Mr Williams told me to get in touch with you. He said you could help us with the organization for our stand at the fair in Boston. You know this will be the first time that we are going to participate in that fair.
Tim Schneider: That's right, Mr Williams informed me about that.
Carlos Lopez: I'm in Munich right now and I would like to meet you and discuss some of the details.
Tim Schneider: That's a good idea. Well, let me see. What about tomorrow morning? Could you manage to come to my office at 10 o'clock?
Carlos Lopez: Yes, that's fine. I'll be there. See you then. Goodbye.
Tim Schneider: Goodbye.

Topic D/f

First call:

Receptionist: Comprints Ltd. Good afternoon.
Ted Wilson: Good afternoon, could I talk to Mr Field, please?
Receptionist: I'm afraid Mr Field is not in the office today.
Ted Wilson: Could you please tell him to call me tomorrow morning? My name is Wilson, Ted Wilson from Vancouver, Canada.
Receptionist: All right Mr Wilson, and your telephone number?
Ted Wilson: I'm calling from London. The number is 404 79 80.
Receptionist: London 404 79 80. I'll tell Mr Field ...

Second call:

Receptionist: Savoy Hotel, good morning.
Angela Parkinson: Good morning, I'd like to talk to Ms Sanders, room 112, please.
Receptionist: Hold the line, please. I'll put you through.
I'm sorry, Madam, but Ms Sanders is not in her room. Would you like to leave a message?

Angela Parkinson:	Yes, please. Tell her to call me back as soon as possible. My name is Angela Parkinson; that's – P.A.R.K.I.N.S.O.N. – and my telephone number is 403 94 79. I'm calling from Berlin. The area code is 30.

Topic E/a

Receptionist:	TFC Boston, can I help you?
Tim Schneider:	Hello, this is Tim Schneider calling from Microware in Munich. I'd like to make a reservation for the PC World Fair this spring. Could you connect me with the person in charge, please?
Receptionist:	Yes, Sir. Hold on, please.
Mary O'Neill:	Hello, Mr Schneider. How are you? I bet you're calling to reserve a stand for the fair next spring.
Tim Schneider:	Yes, we're going to participate again and we'd like to reserve the same stand we had last year as well as the smaller one next to it. We're reserving the smaller stand for Electro Sul, one of our co-operating companies in South America.
Mary O'Neill:	Let me see. Just a moment, Mr Schneider. I'll check to see if your stand is still available. Last year you had stand no. 332. Luckily it's still available. Stand no. 333 next to it is available as well.
Tim Schneider:	I'm glad to hear that. Could you confirm our reservation as soon as possible?
Mary O'Neill:	Certainly. I'll send you a fax this afternoon.
Tim Schneider:	Thank you very much for your help, Ms O' Neill. I look forward to seeing you at the fair.
Mary O'Neill:	Thank's for calling. Goodbye.

Unit 3

Topic A/a

1. Digitext
   PO Box 16
   Birkshaw, BH12 4YX
   England

2. PLYC
   Lower Francis Road
   Dublin 1
   Ireland

3. Tech-Builders
   435 Boyle Street
   Boston, MA 02116
   USA

4. Effective Info
   PO Box A189
   Sydney South NWO 3000
   Australia

5. Micro-Tel
   800 South Wilson Square
   San Francisco CA 95701
   USA

Topic C/g

1. Hello, Ms Birch. This is Kay Tanner from Moto-Van.
   I'm calling about our order no. 849 which we placed on 17 October. It called for delivery of various kinds of fan belts which we really need urgently. You acknow-ledged this order on 20 October and promised us prompt delivery. However, we haven't yet received these supplies and the delay is causing us great inconveni-

ence. If we don't receive the goods by 10 November, we'll have to take our business elsewhere. Please call me concerning this matter as soon as possible. Thanks and goodbye.

2. Good morning, Mr Chi-Loung. This is Stephan Lechner calling from Power Machines in Frankfurt, Germany.
   We are manufacturers and exporters of high-power diesel engines and we're looking for an opportunity to do business in China. Our product range includes engines for ships as well as various other kinds of agricultural, textile and industrial machines. We'd be grateful if you brought our products to the attention of firms with a need for these types of engines. If you'd like more information about our company, please contact the German Chamber of Commerce in Frankfurt. I'd appreciate it if you'd get back to me on this as soon as you can. My telephone number is 069-83760-563.
   Thank you very much. Goodbye.

3. Hello, Mr Brown. Susan McMan speaking, from Al-Water Sprinkler Systems in London.
   Thanks a lot for your recent enquiry regarding our automated sprinkler system. We're very pleased to offer you our services. We'll send you a brochure with information on the technical details, such as the area each unit can service, the amount of water penetrating the soil in a given time, the timer as well as detailed instructions for installing the system. Prices depend on the size of the area to be serviced and vary from £ 2,000 for our smallest unit to £ 10,000 for the largest individual unit. All our prices are usually quoted FOB London. Our terms of payment are by bank draft on receipt of invoice. Let me know if you need any further information concerning our product.

Unit 4

Topic A/a

Tim Schneider: Hello. You must be Mr Thomson. I'm Tim Schneider from Microware. It's a pleasure to meet you. Did you have a good flight?
Mr Thomson: Oh, yes, thank you. A little long, but comfortable.
Tim Schneider: Can I help you with your bags?
Mr Thomson: No, thank you. That's very kind of you but they aren't heavy.
Tim Schneider: My car is in the parking lot. We'll head for the office if that's all right with you. Or would you prefer to go to your hotel first? It's quite near.
Mr Thomson: I would like to go to the office first, really.
Tim Schneider: All right, this way please.

Topic B/a

Tim Schneider: Here we are. Can I take your coat? Mr Brown will be right with you. Please have a seat. Would you like a cup of tea or coffee?
Mr Thomson: Yes, please. Coffee would be nice.

Tim Schneider: How do you like your coffee?
Mr Thomson: Black with sugar, please.
Tim Schneider: Here you are.
Mr Thomson: Thanks a lot.
Tim Schneider: You're welcome. We've booked you into the Bavaria Hotel just up the road. I hope you'll be happy with your accommodation.
Mr Thomson: I'm sure I will.
Tim Schneider: Oh, here's Mr Brown.

Topic C/a

Ms Anderson: This is one of my favourite places for lunch. It's quite near and they serve excellent food here.
Mr Thomson: I'm sure I'll like it. But it's good to have you with me because my German is miserable. I'm afraid you'll have to help me with the menu. I can't read it.
Ms Anderson: Here we are. This table is reserved for us.
Would you like to order a drink first?
Mr Thomson: Yes, I think I'll have a mineral water.
Ms Anderson: And I'll take an orange juice. Herr Ober!
Mr Thomson: How do you call for the waiter in German?
Ms Anderson: You say *Herr Ober*. Now let's have a look at the menu. They have prawn cocktail, tomato soup or hot beef tea as starter.
Mr Thomson: I think I can do without a starter. I'm not very hungry.
Ms Anderson: As a main course you can choose between fish and meat. All dishes are served with rice, chips or roast potatoes and vegetables of the day or salad.
Mr Thomson: What kind of fish do they have?
Ms Anderson: There's rainbow trout and plaice on the menu.
Mr Thomson: And what about meat?
Ms Anderson: The lamb chops are very good. But there's goulash and chicken curry as well. And I can recommend pork fillet or pepper steak.
Mr Thomson: I think I'll have goulash. It's a typical German dish, isn't it?
Ms Anderson: No, not really, but it's very popular in Germany. Well, I'll have the lamb chops. Would you like a beer or do you prefer wine?
Mr Thomson: A beer would be great.
Ms Anderson: We can decide later about the dessert. There's ice cream, mousse au chocolat and a fresh fruit salad. Let's order now.
Herr Ober!

Unit 5

Topic A/d

Angela: Nelson's Travel. Guten Tag.
Miriam: Hello, Angela. This is Miriam Tellmann from Microware in Munich. How are you?
Angela: Hello, Miriam. Fine, thanks. And you?

Miriam:	I'm fine, too, thanks. Two colleagues and myself are flying to Boston for the fair and I would like to book three return flights from Munich to Boston.
Angela:	Oh, lucky you! When would you like to leave?
Miriam:	We would like to be in Boston on May 2nd.
Angela:	And when would you like your return flight?
Miriam:	On May 8th, please.
Angela:	There are no direct flights from Munich to Boston. You would have to change planes in New York. Or you could fly from Frankfurt. There is one direct flight from Frankfurt to Boston daily.
Miriam:	Yes, I think Frankfurt would be better.
Angela:	Okay. Let me see what's available. Which class would you like?
Miriam:	Business class, please.
Angela:	Yes, I have three flights on May 2nd, but I'm afraid the Boston/Frankfurt flight on May 8th is full. Flights are available either on May 7th or on May 9th.
Miriam:	May 9th would be better, I think.
Angela:	Good. You fly out of Frankfurt at 10.20 am. Check-in is an hour earlier. So I'll book you on the 8.05 flight from Munich.
Miriam:	When do we arrive in Boston?
Angela:	You arrive in Boston at 12.10 pm local time. There is a six-hour time difference.
Miriam:	And what about the return flight?
Angela:	You leave Boston at 6.15 pm arriving in Frankfurt at 9.55 am on May 10th. The connection to Munich is no problem. There is a flight at 10.45 am.
Miriam:	That sounds good.
Angela:	Okay. I'll make the booking.
Miriam:	Thanks a lot for your help.
Angela:	You're always welcome. Have a good trip!
Miriam:	Thanks, bye.

Topic C/a

Clerk:	Good morning, Sir. Can I help you?
Passenger:	Yes, please. I'd like a return ticket from London to Birmingham.
Clerk:	Would that be first or second class?
Passenger:	First class, please.
Clerk:	Would you like to reserve a seat?
Passenger:	Yes, I have to be in Birmingham by 1.30 pm tomorrow and would like to return on the first train back to London the next day.
Clerk:	Okay. All right. Would you like an aisle or a window seat?
Passenger:	Aisle seat, please.
Clerk:	Is that smoking or non-smoking?
Passenger:	Non-smoking, please.
Clerk:	Good. I've booked you on the 11.45 train to Birmingham tomorrow morning. The first train from Birmingham to London is at 5.25 am. They go every hour.

Passenger: Oh, well, in that case I think the 7.25 train will be early enough.
Clerk: Right you are, Sir. Here you are. Here is your ticket and your reservation. Have a good trip!
Passenger: Thank you very much and goodbye.

Topic D/b

Tim Schneider: Tim Schneider speaking.
Frank Williams: Good morning, Tim. This is Mr Williams. Could you do me a favour, please? I have to go to Berlin for a meeting tomorrow at 4 pm. I want to take the train. Could you pick up the ticket for me at the station?
Tim Schneider: Sure, Mr Williams. You have to be in Berlin at 4 pm?
Frank Williams: Yes, and it will take about a quarter of an hour by taxi to get to the company from the station.
Tim Schneider: When will you be returning to Munich?
Frank Williams: I'd like to be on the first train out of Berlin the next morning.
Tim Schneider: First or second class?
Frank Williams: I'd like a first class, non-smoking, aisle seat, please.
Tim Schneider: Fine, Mr Williams. I'll bring you the ticket when I get back.
Frank Williams: Thanks Tim, that's a great help.
Tim Schneider: You're welcome.

Topic D/c

Attention, please, all passengers for Berlin! Attention, please, all passengers for Berlin!
Train number ICE 682 Munich to Berlin changing at Fulda, planned departure 7.20 am has been cancelled due to technical difficulties.
I repeat:
Train number ICE 682 Munich to Berlin changing at Fulda, planned departure 7.20 am has been cancelled due to technical difficulties.

Passengers are requested to inquire at the information desk or to check train schedules for the next possible departure to Berlin. We regret any inconvenience caused by this change in schedule. Thank you.

Unit 6

Topic A/b

Receptionist: Good evening. Welcome to the Regent Hotel. May I help you?
Patricia: Yes, Ms O' Neill from TFC Boston has made reservations for us.
Receptionist: And what are your names, please?
Patricia: Ms Newman, Ms Tellmann and Mr Schneider from Microware in Germany.
Receptionist: Yes, I have your reservation here. Your rooms are ready for you. We have three single rooms with a bath booked for you until May 8th. That's six nights.

Patricia: Oh, there must have been a misunderstanding somewhere. We are not returning to Munich until May 9th. We couldn't get an earlier flight.
Receptionist: Well, let me see. No problem. Many of our guests are leaving on the last day of the fair so you can stay in your rooms until May 9th.
Patricia: Oh, that's wonderful!
Receptionist: Would you please fill in the registration forms? Thank you. You have rooms 905, 906 and 907 on the 9th floor. Here are the keys. Check-out time is at 11 am. City tours, if you are interested, leave from here. Tickets are available at the reception. There is a booklet with further information in your rooms. Do you need any help with your luggage?
Patricia: Yes, that would be nice. Oh, I have another question. What about a bus to the fair?
Receptionist: There is a shuttle service which leaves in front of the hotel every hour. The first bus leaves at 6.30 am.
Patricia: And where can I get the bus tickets?
Receptionist: You pay on the bus.
Patricia: Thank you very much for your help.
Receptionist: You're welcome, Madam. Enjoy your stay in Boston.

Topic D/b

Check-in agent: Good afternoon. May I see your tickets, please?
Patricia: Here they are. The three of us would like to sit together if possible.
Check-in agent: Would you like smoking or non-smoking?
Patricia: Non-smoking, please.
Check-in agent: I have window, centre and aisle seats together in row five, non-smoking section. Do you have any luggage to check in?
Patricia: Yes, we have these three suitcases.
Check-in agent: And do you have any hand luggage?
Patricia: We've got two flight bags and a handbag.
Check-in agent: Okay. The airport security charge is $5 each.
Patricia: That's $15 altogether. Here you are.
Check-in agent: Thank you, Madam. Here are your tickets. The baggage claim check is attached to the back of each ticket. And here are your boarding cards. Boarding time is 5.30 at gate 14. Enjoy your flight!
Patricia: Thank you. Goodbye.
Check-in agent: Don't forget your tickets!

Unit 7

Topic C/e

Interviewer: Hi, and welcome to "You & Yours". On today's programme we look at two European school systems in comparison, Great Britain and France. In both school systems education is compulsory till the age of 16.

With me in the studio I'd like to welcome Susan Beach from London who works in an infant school during the day, and studies languages at the University of London in the evening.
Susan, nice to have you with us this morning. Could you tell us something about how the English state school system is organized.

Susan: Well, in Great Britain children can go to nursery or pre-primary school at the age of two. Primary school then begins for each child after he or she has turned five. Primary school itself is divided into infant school and junior school. Secondary education begins at the age of 11 in a comprehensive school.
However, pupils can attend a secondary school or a traditional grammar school.
At the age of 16, pupils take the GCSE examination, which used to be called "O" Levels or CSEs. Pupils who have taken the GCSE examination can either go into Youth Training Schemes, take a job which does not require any kind of training or continue with full-time education to prepare themselves for training in different fields.
Those pupils who decide to study for another two years, take the GCE "A" Level examination, which allows them entry to colleges and universities.

Interviewer: Thank you very much, Susan. And now to our next guest, Françoise Duval from Paris. Françoise is studying for her baccalauréat and then wants to go on to the university to study medicine.
Hi, Françoise and welcome to today's "You & Yours". Françoise, how does the French education system work?

Françoise: In France compulsory education begins at the age of six and ends at the age of 16. However, most children attend a nursery school (école maternelle) between the age of two and six. That's where they get their first pre-school education.
Ecole élémentaire begins when the child is six years old. After attending the école élémentaire for five years the pupils enter a four-year secondary school. It is a type of comprehensive school with different class levels based on pupils' assessments, choice of foreign languages or particular aptitude. At the end of their four years (in the troisième) the pupils take an examination. This exam determines which academic or vocational course of studies the pupil can take. The student, based on his or her ability can either attend a three-year lycée (general or technical); a two-year lycée, which prepares for different professions, or students can decide on an apprenticeship, which usually takes two or three years. Only those attending the three-year lycée can gain entry to university, provided they pass the baccalauréat examination.

Interviewer: That all sounds very interesting. Thank you very much, Françoise.
Thanks everybody for joining us today. Next on "You & Yours" we look at children who are trying to be champions in the world of sport. Till next week, bye!

Unit 8

Topic C/a

Jack Artner: Good afternoon, Mr Schneider. My name is Artner.
Tim Schneider: Nice to meet you, Mr Artner.
Jack Artner: How was the train journey to Frankfurt, Mr Schneider?
Tim Schneider: Thank you, fine. It was quite relaxing.
Jack Artner: Mr Schneider, what are your reasons for applying for a position with our company?
Tim Schneider: I've been interested in the development of software for quite some time now and your company has become one of the leaders in this field here in Germany. I believe that the post offers great career opportunities. And I don't see any of those opportunities in my present job.
Jack Artner: What qualifications do you have that make you think you'll be successful in the area of marketing?
Tim Schneider: I'm open to new ideas and I've always kept myself informed about the latest trends in marketing. Furthermore, my experience at C-Base and Microware has given me an insight into the needs of commercial customers.
Jack Artner: Thinking back over your career, what have you enjoyed most and what least?
Tim Schneider: I enjoyed particularly dealing with our customers as well as with our suppliers. Working with the producers kept me informed on the latest developments and this again helped me to give our customers the best advice. Least of all I enjoyed paperwork such as filing and compiling records.
Jack Artner: In what way do you feel that you've been most effective in your work?
Tim Schneider: Contacting new customers and recommending as well as promoting new products.
Jack Artner: How has your educational background prepared you for a career in marketing?
Tim Schneider: I have a solid background in computer science, financial planning, calculation, accounting, computing and analysis of data and I was also trained in management and marketing strategies.
Jack Artner: What has been your most rewarding experience so far?
Tim Schneider: I think that was receiving a prize in computer science two years ago. I worked on a programme which I improved to better suit the company's needs.
Jack Artner: What have you learned from participation in extra-curricular activities?
Tim Schneider: Playing in a local football team has been a lot of fun and, of course, helped me to develop team spirit.
Jack Artner: Hm, good. Before I provide you with some additional information about the job, what else should I know about you in order to make the best possible employment decision?

Tim Schneider: I would like to stress again that I work well in a group. However, if necessary, I'm quite capable of making decisions on my own. My past experience shows you that my work has always been based on initiative and willingness to work no matter how difficult the task may be.

Jack Artner: Well, do you have any questions?

Tim Schneider: Yes, I'd really like to know some more details about your company...

Contextual vocabulary

Unitbegleitendes Wörterverzeichnis

Dieses Wörterverzeichnis enthält in chronologischer Reihenfolge Wörter und Wendungen aus den Units 1 bis 8. Die deutschen Übersetzungen beziehen sich auf den jeweiligen Unitkontext. Ein Grundwortschatz von ungefähr 2.000 Wörtern wird als bekannt vorausgesetzt.

Zum schnelleren Auffinden von Wörtern und Wendungen gibt es im Anschluss an das unitbegleitende Wörterverzeichnis ein alphabetisches Wortregister. Es enthält alle Wörter aus dem unitbegleitenden Wörterverzeichnis. Die Buchstaben hinter den Einträgen geben die jeweilige Fundstelle an (z.B. 1, Ab = Unit 1, Topic A, exercise b).

Folgende Abkürzungen werden im Wörterverzeichnis verwendet:

adj.	= adjective (Eigenschaftswort)	*n.*	= noun (Substantiv, Hauptwort)
adv.	= adverb (Umstandswort)	*pl.*	= plural (Mehrzahl)
AE	= American English	*s.o.*	= someone (jemand)
BE	= British English	*s.th.*	= something (etwas)
inf.	= informal (umgangssprachlich)	*v.*	= verb (Zeitwort)

Phonetic alphabet · Lautschrift

[ː] bedeutet, dass der vorangegangene Laut lang ist
[ˈ] bedeutet, dass die folgende Silbe eine Hauptbetonung erhält
[ˌ] bedeutet, dass die folgende Silbe eine Nebenbetonung erhält
[‿] bedeutet, dass die beiden Laute miteinander verbunden werden

[iː]	meet [miːt]	[eɪ]	name [neɪm]	[f]	fine [faɪn]
[ɑː]	father [ˈfɑːðə]	[aɪ]	my [maɪ]	[v]	evening [ˈiːvnɪŋ]
[ɔː]	morning [ˈmɔːnɪŋ]	[ɔɪ]	toilet [ˈtɔɪlɪt]	[θ]	thanks [θæŋks]
[uː]	school [skuːl]	[əʊ]	phone [fəʊn]	[ð]	this [ðɪs]
[ɜː]	firm [fɜːm]	[aʊ]	now [naʊ]	[s]	son [sʌn]
		[ɪə]	beer [bɪə]	[z]	is [ɪz]
[ɪ]	in [ɪn]	[eə]	where [weə]	[ʃ]	she [ʃiː]
[e]	yes [jes]	[ʊə]	tourist [ˈtʊərɪst]	[ʒ]	television [ˈtelɪˌvɪʒn]
[æ]	thanks [θæŋks]			[h]	he [hiː]
[ʌ]	much [mʌtʃ]	[p]	pub [pʌb]	[m]	my [maɪ]
[ɒ]	what [wɒt]	[b]	bye [baɪ]	[n]	now [naʊ]
[ʊ]	good [gʊd]	[t]	town [taʊn]	[ŋ]	evening [ˈiːvnɪŋ]
[ə]	number [ˈnʌmbə]	[d]	drink [drɪŋk]	[l]	like [laɪk]
		[k]	coffee [ˈkɒfɪ]	[r]	room [rʊm]
		[g]	good [gʊd]	[w]	we [wiː]
		[tʃ]	church [tʃɜːtʃ]	[j]	yes [jes]
		[dʒ]	job [dʒɒb]		

Unit 1

A

department	[dɪ'pɑːtmənt]	Abteilung
London-based	['lʌndn ˌbeɪst]	in London ansässig
Munich	['mjuːnɪk]	München
marketing assistant	['mɑːkɪtɪŋ‿ə'sɪstənt]	Mitarbeiter/in i.d. Marketingabteilung
marketing department	['mɑːkɪtɪŋ dɪ'pɑːtmənt]	Marketingabteilung

Aa

look like	[lʊk‿laɪk]	aussehen wie, ähneln

Ab

be in charge of	[biː‿ɪn 'tʃɑːdʒ‿əv]	verantwortlich sein für
position	[pə'zɪʃn]	Stellung, Position

Ac

show s.o. around	[ʃəʊ 'sʌmwʌn‿ə'raʊnd]	jdn. herumführen
co-worker	[ˌkəʊ'wɜːkə]	Kollege, Kollegin
closely *(adv.)*	['kləʊslɪ]	eng, nah
sales department	['seɪlz dɪ'pɑːtmənt]	Verkaufsabteilung
advertising department	['ædvətaɪzɪŋ dɪ'pɑːtmənt]	Werbeabteilung
get settled in (job)	[get 'setld‿ɪn]	sich eingewöhnen, einleben
get back	[get bæk]	wiederkommen, zurückkommen
hesitate	['hezɪteɪt]	zögern
organization chart	[ˌɔːgənaɪ'zeɪʃn tʃɑːt]	Organigramm
chart	[tʃɑːt]	Tabelle, Plan
personnel department	[ˌpɜːsə'nel dɪ'pɑːtmənt]	Personalabteilung
research and development department	['riːsɜːtʃ‿ən‿dɪ'veləpmənt dɪ'pɑːtmənt]	Forschungs- und Entwicklungsabteilung
research manager	['riːsɜːtʃ 'mænɪdʒə]	Leiter/in d. Forschungsabteilung
sales manager	[seɪlz 'mænɪdʒə]	Leiter/in d. Verkaufsabteilung
finance department	[faɪ'næns dɪ'pɑːtmənt]	Finanzabteilung
chief accountant	[tʃiːf‿ə'kaʊntənt]	Chefbuchhalter/in

Ae

match *(v.)*	[mætʃ]	*hier:* zuordnen

Ba

item	['aɪtəm]	Gegenstand
filing cabinet	['faɪlɪŋ‿'kæbɪnət]	Aktenschrank
in-tray	['ɪntreɪ]	Posteingangsablage
out-tray	['aʊttreɪ]	Postausgangsablage
notice board	['nəʊtɪs‿bɔːd]	Anschlagbrett, „schwarzes Brett“
wastepaper basket	[ˌweɪst'peɪpəˌbɑːskɪt]	Papierkorb
stapler	['steɪplə]	Hefter, Heftmaschine

hole punch	[həʊl pʌntʃ]	Locher
photocopier	['fəʊtəʊˌkɒpɪə]	Fotokopiergerät
answering machine	['ɑːnsərɪŋ‿mə'ʃiːn]	Anrufbeantworter

Bb

workplace	['wɜːkpleɪs]	Arbeitsplatz
get on well	[get‿ɒn wel]	sich gut verstehen
survey *(n.)*	['sɜːveɪ]	Bericht, Studie
date back	[deɪt bæk]	zurückliegen, zurückdatieren
operate	['ɒpəreɪt]	bedienen, betätigen
by the way	[baɪ ðə 'weɪ]	übrigens
powdered milk	['paʊdəd mɪlk]	Milchpulver

Bf

typing paper	['taɪpɪŋ 'peɪpə]	Schreibmaschinenpapier
extension (number)	[ɪk'stenʃn‿'nʌmbə]	Durchwahl

Ca

request *(n.)*	[rɪ'kwest]	Bitte, Nachfrage
response	[rɪ'spɒns]	Antwort, Erwiderung

Cc

book *(v.)*	[bʊk]	reservieren (lassen), buchen
word lobster	[wɜːd 'lɒbstə]	Wortnetz
lobster	['lɒbstə]	Hummer
bother *(n.)*	['bɒðə]	Mühe, Belastung

Ce

occasionally	[ə'keɪʒənəlɪ]	gelegentlich

D

corridor	['kɒrɪdɔː]	Gang, Korridor
lounge	[laʊndʒ]	Empfangsraum, Aufenthaltsraum
canteen	[kæn'tiːn]	Kantine
Ladies' (room)	['leɪdɪz‿ruːm]	Damentoilette
Gents'	[dʒents]	Herrentoilette
elevator *(AE)*	['eləveɪtə]	Fahrstuhl, Aufzug
stationery	['steɪʃənrɪ]	Schreibwaren
receptionist	[rɪ'sepʃənɪst]	Empfangsdame, Empfangschef
data processing	['deɪtə ˌprəʊsesɪŋ]	Datenverarbeitung
storage	['stɔːrɪdʒ]	Lagerung
conference room	['kɒnfərəns‿ruːm]	Konferenzzimmer, -raum

Db

reception desk	[rɪ'sepʃn desk]	Empfangsschalter

Dc

directions *(pl.)*	[dɪ'rekʃnz]	Wegbeschreibung

Unit 2

Aa

receive a phone call	[rɪ'si:v‿ə 'fəʊnkɔ:l]	einen Anruf bekommen
polite	[pə'laɪt]	höflich
agreeable	[ə'grɪəbl]	angenehm, zustimmend
brief	[bri:f]	kurz, knapp
have s.th. at hand	[hæv 'sʌmθɪŋ‿ət hænd]	etw. zur Hand haben
confirm	[kən'fɜ:m]	bestätigen
precisely *(adv.)*	[prɪ'saɪslɪ]	genau, exakt

Ab

look s.th. up	[lʊk 'sʌmθɪŋ‿ʌp]	etw. nachschlagen
pick up	[pɪk‿ʌp]	*hier:* (den Hörer) abnehmen
international code	[ˌɪntə'næʃənl kəʊd]	Ländervorwahl
long-distance call	['lɒŋˌdɪstəns kɔ:l]	Ferngespräch
telephone directory	['teləfəʊn dɪ'rektərɪ]	Telefonbuch
local call	['ləʊkl kɔ:l]	Ortsgespräch
receiver	[rɪ'si:və]	Telefonhörer
area code	['eərɪə kəʊd]	Ortsnetzkennzahl
engaged *(BE)*, busy *(AE)*	[ɪn'geɪdʒd / 'bɪzɪ]	besetzt (Telefonleitung)

Ba

put s.o. through	[pʊt 'sʌmwʌn θru:]	jdn. verbinden (Telefon)
Hold the line, please.	[həʊld‿ðə 'laɪn pli:z]	Bleiben Sie bitte am Apparat.
leave a message	[li:v ə 'mesɪdʒ]	eine Nachricht hinterlassen

Bd

appropriate	[ə'prəʊprɪət]	passend, angemessen

Bg

imaginary	[ɪ'mædʒɪnərɪ]	imaginär, vorgestellt

C

make arrangements	[meɪk ə'reɪndʒmənts]	Vorbereitungen, Verabredungen treffen

Ca

participate in	[pɑ:'tɪsɪpeɪt ɪn]	teilnehmen an
fair *(n.)*	[feə]	Messe, Ausstellung
get in touch	[get ɪn tʌtʃ]	sich in Verbindung setzen
stand *(n.)*	[stænd]	Stand (auf der Messe)

Cb

staff meeting	[stɑ:f 'mi:tɪŋ]	Mitarbeiterversammlung

Cc

market research	['mɑ:kɪt 'ri:sɜ:tʃ]	Marktforschung
mum *(inf. for mother)*	[mʌm]	Mami, Mutti

Cd

flowchart	['fləʊtʃɑːt]	Flussdiagramm
guide *(n.)*	[gaɪd]	*hier:* Anhaltspunkt, Modell

Ce

spend (time)	[spend taɪm]	(Zeit) verbringen

Dd

punctuation mark	[ˌpʌŋktʃʊ'eɪʃn mɑːk]	Satzzeichen
quotation marks, inverted commas	[kwəʊ'teɪʃn mɑːks / ɪn'vɜːtɪd 'kɒməz]	Anführungszeichen
exclamation mark	[ˌekskləˈmeɪʃn mɑːk]	Ausrufezeichen
dash	[dæʃ]	Gedankenstrich
full stop *(BE)*/ period *(AE)*	[fʊl stɒp / 'pɪərɪəd]	Punkt (Satzende)
hyphen	['haɪfn]	Bindestrich
colon	['kəʊlɒn]	Doppelpunkt
stroke *(BE)*/slash *(AE)*	[strəʊk / slæʃ]	Strich
(round) brackets	[raʊnd 'brækɪts]	(runde) Klammern
parentheses *(pl.)*	[pə'renθɪsiːz]	Klammer(zeichen)
question mark	['kwestʃn mɑːk]	Fragezeichen
(square) brackets	[skweə 'brækɪts]	(eckige) Klammern

De

opening hours	['əʊpnɪŋ‿ˌaʊəz]	Öffnungszeit(en)
BA = British Airways	[ˌbiː'eɪ ˌbrɪtɪʃ 'eəweɪz]	
delayed	[dɪ'leɪd]	verspätet

Ea

bet *(v.)*	[bet]	wetten
available	[ə'veɪləbl]	zur Verfügung stehen

Eb

take place	[teɪk pleɪs]	stattfinden
promise *(v.)*	['prɒmɪs]	versprechen

Ee

apply	[ə'plaɪ]	*hier:* beantragen
calling card	['kɔːlɪŋ kɑːd]	Telefonkarte
access *(v.)*	['ækses]	*hier:* erreichen, sich in Verbindung setzen mit
operator	['ɒpəreɪtə]	Vermittlung (Telefon)
conference call	['kɒnfərəns kɔːl]	Telefonkonferenz
economical	[ˌiːkə'nɒmɪkl]	wirtschaftlich, sparsam
itemized	['aɪtəmaɪzd]	aufgeschlüsselt (nach Anrufen)

Unit 3

A

correspondence	[ˌkɒrɪˈspɒndəns]	Korrespondenz
concerning	[kənˈsɜːnɪŋ]	betreffend
present *(v.)*	[prɪˈzent]	präsentieren, vorstellen
postcode *(BE)*, ZIP code *(AE)*	[ˈpəʊstkəʊd /ˈzɪpkəʊd]	Postleitzahl

Aa

address *(v.)*	[əˈdres]	adressieren

Ab

abbreviation	[əˌbriːvɪˈeɪʃn]	Abkürzung
reference	[ˈrefrəns]	Bezug
salutation	[ˌsæljuːˈteɪʃn]	Grußformel
body of letter	[ˈbɒdɪ‿əv ˈletə]	Brieftext
reason *(n.)*	[ˈriːzn]	Grund, Anlass
closing sentence	[ˈkləʊzɪŋ ˈsentəns]	Schlusssatz
complimentary close	[ˌkɒmplɪˈmentərɪ kləʊz]	Schluss-, Grußformel
enclosure	[ɪnˈkləʊʒə]	Anlage (Brief)
return address	[rɪˈtɜːn‿əˈdres]	Rückadresse
distributor	[dɪˈstrɪbjʊtə]	Vertrieb, Händler/in
high speed modem	[ˌhaɪˈspiːd ˈməʊdem]	Hochgeschwindigkeitsmodem
in view of	[ɪn ˈvjuː‿əv]	angesichts
range *(n.)*	[reɪndʒ]	*hier:* Produktpalette
approved	[əˈpruːvd]	*hier:* genehmigt
appreciate	[əˈpriːʃɪeɪt]	schätzen, würdigen
bring s.th. to the attention of s.o.	[brɪŋˈsʌmθɪŋ tʊ‿ðɪ‿əˈtenʃn‿əv ˈsʌmwʌn]	jdn. auf etw. aufmerksam machen
large-scale user	[ˈlɑːdʒˌskeɪl ˈjuːzə]	Großanwender
distribute	[dɪˈstrɪbjuːt]	vertreiben, verteilen
potential supplier	[pəˈtenʃl səˈplaɪə]	potentieller Lieferant
quotation	[kwəʊˈteɪʃn]	Angebot, Kostenvoranschlag
initial order	[ɪˈnɪʃl‿ˈɔːdə]	Erstauftrag

Ad

enquiry	[ɪnˈkwaɪərɪ]	Anfrage

Ae

demand *(n.)*	[dɪˈmɑːnd]	Nachfrage
innovative	[ˈɪnəvətɪv]	innovativ

Ba

agency agreement	[ˈeɪdʒənsɪ‿əˈgriːmənt]	Vertreter-, Agenturvertrag
discount *(n.)*	[ˈdɪskaʊnt]	Rabatt, Skonto
sales agreement	[seɪlz‿əˈgriːmənt]	Kaufvertrag
printed material	[ˈprɪntɪd məˈtɪərɪəl]	Informationsmaterial
delivery date	[dɪˈlɪvərɪ deɪt]	Liefertermin

terms of delivery and payment	[tɜːmz‿əv dɪ'lɪvərɪ‿ənd 'peɪmənt]	Liefer- und Zahlungsbedingungen
quote *(v.)*	[kwəʊt]	Angebot unterbreiten
packing	['pækɪŋ]	Verpackung
grant a discount	[grɑːnt‿ə 'dɪskaʊnt]	einen Rabatt gewähren
effect *(v.)*	[ɪ'fekt]	durch-, ausführen
surrender documents	sə'rendə 'dɒkjʊmənts]	Dokumente aushändigen
bank acceptance	[bæŋk‿ək'septəns]	Bankakzept
take advantage	[teɪk‿əd'vɑːntɪdʒ]	einen Vorteil nutzen
favourable *(BE)*, favorable *(AE)*	['feɪvrəbl]	günstig

Bb

submit (a quotation)	[sʌb'mɪt‿ə kwəʊ'teɪʃn]	(ein Angebot) unterbreiten, vorlegen
specify	['spesɪfaɪ]	angeben, spezifizieren
leaflet	['liːflɪt]	Prospekt, Informationsblatt
supply from stock	[sə'plaɪ frəm stɒk]	ab Lager liefern
optional	['ɒpʃənl]	wahlfrei

Bc

remain	[rɪ'meɪn]	(übrig) bleiben

C

delay *(n.)*	[dɪ'leɪ]	Verzögerung, Verspätung

Ca

order form	['ɔːdə fɔːm]	Bestellformular
place an order	[pleɪs‿ən‿'ɔːdə]	einen Auftrag erteilen
competitive	[kəm'petətɪv]	wettbewerbsfähig
rapidly developing	['ræpɪdlɪ dɪ'veləpɪŋ]	schnell entwickelnd
trust *(v.)*	[trʌst]	vertrauen
prompt *(adj.)*	[prɒmt]	unverzüglich, umgehend
acknowledgement	[ək'nɒlɪdʒmənt]	(Empfangs)Bestätigung

Cb

introductory phrase	[ˌɪntrə'dʌktərɪ freɪz]	Einleitungssatz
confirmation	[ˌkɒnfə'meɪʃn]	Bestätigung

Cd

immediate delivery	[ɪ'miːdjət dɪ'lɪvərɪ]	unverzügliche Lieferung
receipt	[rɪ'siːt]	Eingang, Empfang
reference	['refrəns]	*hier:* Referenz(schreiben)
energy efficient	['enədʒɪ‿ɪ'fɪʃənt]	energiesparend
lightbulb	['laɪtbʌlb]	Glühbirne
be forced	[biː fɔːst]	gezwungen sein
obtain	[əb'teɪn]	erhalten, bekommen, beziehen

Ce

apologize	[ə'pɒlədʒaɪz]	sich entschuldigen
hold s.o. liable for	[həʊld 'sʌmwʌn 'laɪəbl fɔː]	jdn. für etw. haftbar machen
loss	[lɒs]	Verlust
be obliged	[biː ə'blaɪdʒd]	gezwungen sein

Cf

legally binding	['liːgəlɪ 'baɪndɪŋ]	rechtlich bindend

Unit 4

A

accompany	[ə'kʌmpənɪ]	begleiten

Aa

uncomfortable	[ʌn'kʌmftəbl]	unangenehm, ungemütlich
parking lot *(AE)*	['pɑːkɪŋ lɒt]	Parkplatz
head for *(v.)*	[hed fɔː]	gehen, fahren zu/nach

Ab

I'd rather ...	[aɪd‿'rɑːðə]	Ich möchte/würde lieber ...

Ac

baggage claim	['bægɪdʒ kleɪm]	Gepäckausgabe
transfer *(n.)*	['trænsfɜː]	Transfer, Transport
domestic flight	[də'mestɪk flaɪt]	Inlandsflug
arrival	[ə'raɪvl]	Ankunft
departure	[dɪ'pɑːtʃə]	Abflug, Abfahrt
customs *(pl.)*	['kʌstəmz]	Zoll
trolley	['trɒlɪ]	Gepäck-, Handwagen
cabin crew	['kæbɪn kruː]	Bordpersonal
refreshments *(pl.)*	[rɪ'freʃmənts]	(kleine) Erfrischungen
bumpy	['bʌmpɪ]	(Flug) böig, unruhig
on time	[ɒn taɪm]	pünktlich

Ba

have a seat	[hæv‿ə 'siːt]	Platz nehmen
Here you are.	['hɪə jʊ‿ɑː]	Bitte./Bittesehr. (wenn man jdm. etw. überreicht)
accommodation	[əˌkɒmə'deɪʃn]	Unterkunft
market *(v.)*	['mɑːkɪt]	vermarkten

C

take s.o. out to lunch	[teɪk 'sʌmwʌn‿aʊt tʊ 'lʌntʃ]	mit jdm. zum Mittagessen ausgehen

Ca

starter *(BE)*	['stɑːtə]	Vorspeise
goulash	['guːlæʃ]	Gulasch
dessert	[dɪ'zɜːt]	Dessert, Nachtisch

Cb

miserable	[ˈmɪzrəbl]	miserabel
mineral water	[ˈmɪnərəl ˈwɔːtə]	Mineralwasser
orange juice	[ˈɒrɪndʒ‿dʒuːs]	Orangensaft
prawn cocktail	[prɔːn ˈkɒkteɪl]	Krabbencocktail
tomato soup	[təˈmɑːtəʊ suːp]	Tomatensuppe
hot beef tea	[hɒt biːf tiː]	heiße Rinderkraftbrühe
main course	[meɪn kɔːs]	Hauptgang, Hauptgericht
rainbow trout	[ˈreɪnbəʊ traʊt]	Regenbogenforelle
plaice	[pleɪs]	Scholle
lamb chop	[læm tʃɒp]	Lammkotelett
pork fillet	[pɔːk ˈfɪlɪt]	Schweinefilet

Cc

wholemeal bread	[ˈhəʊlmiːl bred]	Vollkornbrot
garlic	[ˈgɑːlɪk]	Knoblauch
mushroom	[ˈmʌʃruːm]	Pilz, Champignon
smoked salmon	[sməʊkt ˈsæmən]	Räucherlachs
shrimp	[ʃrɪmp]	Garnele, Krabbe
sauté	[ˈsəʊteɪ]	(kurz) gebraten, geröstet
scampi	[ˈskæmpɪ]	Scampi
herb sauce	[hɜːb sɔːs]	Kräutersoße
veal cutlet	[vɪəl ˈkʌtlɪt]	Kalbsschnitzel
roast turkey	[rəʊst ˈtɜːkɪ]	Puterbraten
cauliflower	[ˈkɒlɪˌflaʊə]	Blumenkohl
corn	[kɔːn]	Mais, Maiskolben
salad garnish	[ˈsæləd ˈgɑːnɪʃ]	Salatgarnitur
selection	[səˈlekʃn]	Auswahl
tip *(n.)*	[tɪp]	Trinkgeld
VAT (Value Added Tax)	[ˌviːˌeɪˈtiː ˌvæljuː‿ˌædɪd ˈtæks]	Mehrwertsteuer

Cd

poultry	[ˈpəʊltrɪ]	Geflügel
seafood	[ˈsiːfuːd]	Meeresfrüchte
lettuce	[ˈletɪs]	Kopfsalat
pineapple	[ˈpaɪnˌæpl]	Ananas
grape	[greɪp]	Weintraube
duck	[dʌk]	Ente
cutlet steak	[ˈkʌtlɪt steɪk]	Hacksteak
kidney pie	[ˈkɪdnɪ paɪ]	Pastete mit Nieren
sole salmon	[səʊl ˈsæmən]	Seezunge
peach	[piːtʃ]	Pfirsich
cucumber	[ˈkjuːkʌmbə]	(Salat)gurke
haddock	[ˈhædək]	Schellfisch
cabbage	[ˈkæbɪdʒ]	Kohl
cod steak	[kɒd steɪk]	Kabeljaufilet
apple pie	[ˈæpl paɪ]	Apfelpastete, Apfelkuchen

Cf

vegetarian *(n.)*	[ˌvedʒəˈteərɪən]	Vegetarier/in

Da

extract *(n.)*	[ˈekstrækt]	Auszug, Ausschnitt
sights *(pl.)*	[saɪts]	Sehenswürdigkeiten
downtown *(AE)*	[ˈdaʊntaʊn]	Innenstadt
get around	[get əˈraʊnd]	herumkommen, umherreisen
underground *(BE)*	[ˈʌndəgraʊnd]	U-Bahn
exhibition	[ˌeksɪˈbɪʃn]	Ausstellung
restauration works	[ˌrestəˈreɪʃn wɜːks]	Restaurationsarbeiten, Renovierung
cuckoo clock	[ˈkʊkuːklɒk]	Kuckucksuhr
doll	[dɒl]	Puppe
speciality	[ˌspeʃɪˈælətɪ]	Spezialität

Db

admission fee	[ədˈmɪʃn fiː]	Eintrittsgeld

Dd

travelcard	[ˈtrævlkɑːd]	Netzkarte zu günstigen Preisen
price reduction	[praɪs rɪˈdʌkʃn]	Preisermäßigung
change *(n.)*	[tʃeɪndʒ]	*hier:* Wechselgeld
fare	[feə]	Fahrpreis
affordable	[əˈfɔːdəbl]	bezahlbar
endlessly convenient	[ˈendləslɪ kənˈviːnɪənt]	*etwa:* ungemein praktisch
zonal system	[ˈzəʊnl ˈsɪstəm]	Fahrpreiszonen-System
... and you're off	[ənd‿jʊər‿ˈɒf]	... und auf geht's
newsagent	[ˈnjuːzˌeɪdʒənt]	Zeitschriftenhändler/in

De

map *(n.)*	[mæp]	Stadtplan, *hier:* Karte des U-Bahnnetzes
fleamarket	[ˈfliːˌmɑːkɪt]	Flohmarkt
westbound	[ˈwestbaʊnd]	in Richtung Westen
eastbound	[ˈiːstbaʊnd]	in Richtung Osten
change *(v.)*	[tʃeɪndʒ]	*hier:* umsteigen

Unit 5

business trip	[ˈbɪznɪs trɪp]	Geschäftsreise

Ad

colleague	[ˈkɒliːg]	Kollege, Kollegin
return flight	[rɪˈtɜːn flaɪt]	Rückflug
sound *(v.)*	[saʊnd]	sich anhören
That sounds good.	[ðæt saʊndz gʊd]	Das klingt gut.

Ae

depart	[dɪ'pɑːt]	abreisen, *hier:* abfliegen
arrival time	[ə'raɪvl taɪm]	Ankunftszeit

Af

jet lag	['dʒetlæg]	Jet-lag, Probleme mit der Zeitverschiebung bei Flugreisen

Ba

reservation	[ˌrezə'veɪʃn]	Reservierung
lobby	['lɒbɪ]	Eingangshalle, Foyer

Bc

ring up	[rɪŋ‿ʌp]	anrufen
require	[rɪ'kwaɪə]	fordern, verlangen
fully booked	['fʊlɪ bʊkt]	ausgebucht
all day	[ɔːl deɪ]	den ganzen Tag (lang)

Bd

facilities *(pl.)*	[fə'sɪlətɪz]	Einrichtungen, Anlagen
hourly	['aʊəlɪ]	stündlich
fairground	['feəgraʊnd]	Messegelände
heated swimming pool	['hiːtɪd 'swɪmɪŋpuːl]	beheiztes Schwimmbad
fully-equipped	['fʊlɪ‿ɪ'kwɪpt]	komplett ausgestattet, vollständig eingerichtet
room service	['ruːm ˌsɜːvɪs]	Zimmerservice
boutique	[buː'tiːk]	Boutique
sauna	['sɔːnə]	Sauna
secretarial service	[ˌsekrə'teərɪəl 'sɜːvɪs]	Sekretär(innen)dienst

Be

design *(v.)*	[dɪ'zaɪn]	entwerfen, planen
location	[ləʊ'keɪʃn]	Lage, Standort

Ca

aisle seat	[aɪl siːt]	Sitz am Gang

Cc

Channel Tunnel	['tʃænl 'tʌnl]	Tunnel unter dem Ärmelkanal

Cd

overnight	[ˌəʊvə'naɪt]	über Nacht

De

visa	['viːzə]	Visum
valid	['vælɪd]	gültig
expire	[ɪk'spaɪə]	ablaufen, verfallen (Datum)
bomb threat	[bɒm θret]	Bombendrohung

Df

be faced with a problem	[biː feɪst wɪð‿ə 'prɒbləm]	mit einem Problem konfrontiert sein

Unit 6

Ab

solution	[sə'lu:ʃn]	Lösung
next to each other	[nekst‿tʊ‿i:tʃ‿'ʌðə]	nebeneinander
shuttle bus	['ʃʌtl bʌs]	Pendelbus

Ac

tennis court	['tenɪskɔ:t]	Tennisplatz
cable TV	['keɪbl ˌti:'vi:]	Kabelfernsehen
interpreter	[ɪn'tɜ:prɪtə]	Dolmetscher/in
computer rental	[kəm'pju:tə‿ˌrentl]	Computervermietung, -verleih
car rental	['kɑ:‿ˌrentl]	Autovermietung
balcony	['bælkənɪ]	Balkon
massage *(n.)*	['mæsɑ:dʒ]	Massage
bureau de change *(BE)*	[bjʊˌrəʊdə'ʃɑ:ŋʒ]	Wechselstube
courier	['kʊrɪə]	Kurier, Eilbote
laundry	['lɔ:ndrɪ]	Wäscherei
dry cleaning	[ˌdraɪ'kli:nɪŋ]	chemisch reinigen

Ad

difference of opinion	['dɪfrəns‿əv‿ə'pɪnjən]	Meinungsunterschied
all-night work session	[ˌɔ:l'naɪt 'wɜ:k‿ˌseʃn]	nächtliche Arbeitssitzung
relax	[rɪ'læks]	(sich) entspannen

Ae

coffee stain	['kɒfɪ steɪn]	Kaffeefleck
currency exchange *(AE)*	['kʌrənsɪ‿ɪks'tʃeɪndʒ]	Wechselstube
remove	[rɪ'mu:v]	entfernen, beseitigen
early-morning call	[ˌɜ:lɪ‿ˌmɔ:nɪŋ‿'kɔ:l]	Weckanruf (Hotel)
car hire service	['kɑ: ˌhaɪə 'sɜ:vɪs]	Autovermietungsdienst
reduced price	[rɪ'dju:st praɪs]	ermäßigter Preis

B

trade fair	[treɪd feə]	Messe, Fachmesse
exhibition hall	[ˌeksɪ'bɪʃn hɔ:l]	Ausstellungshalle
press conference	['pres‿ˌkɒnfərəns]	Pressekonferenz

Ba

a bit	[ə bɪt]	ein wenig, etwas
ship *(v.)*	[ʃip]	versenden, schicken
by mistake	[ˌbaɪ‿mɪs'teɪk]	irrtümlich
brochure	['brəʊʃə]	Broschüre, Prospekt
rest *(n.)*	[rest]	Rest
lunchtime	['lʌntʃtaɪm]	Mittagszeit (gegen 13 Uhr)
stuff	[stʌf]	Zeug, *hier:* Material, Ausrüstung
freshen up	['freʃn‿ʌp]	(sich) erfrischen
be accustomed to s.th.	[bɪ‿ə'kʌstəmd‿tʊ 'sʌmθɪŋ]	gewöhnt sein, etw. zu tun
routine	[ru:'ti:n]	Routine

discover	[dɪ'skʌvə]	entdecken, feststellen
mess	[mes]	Durcheinander, Chaos
Oh dear!	[ˌəʊ‿'dɪə]	Meine Güte!

Bb

state *(n.)*	[steɪt]	Zustand
event	[ɪ'vent]	Ereignis

Be

emphasis	['emfəsɪs]	Nachdruck, Gewicht
bold type	[bəʊld‿taɪp]	Fettdruck

Bf

press release	['pres‿rɪˌliːs]	Pressemitteilung
issue *(v.)*	['ɪʃuː]	herausgeben, veröffentlichen
consulting *(n.)*	[kən'sʌltɪŋ]	Beratung
trend	[trend]	Tendenz, Trend
in recent years	[ɪn 'riːsnt 'jɪəz]	in den letzten Jahren
exhibitor	[eg'zɪbɪtə]	Aussteller/in
updated version	[ˌʌp'deɪtɪd 'vɜːʃn]	neueste Version
feature *(n.)*	['fiːtʃə]	Merkmal, Eigenschaft
promote	[prə'məʊt]	werben für
customized	['kʌstəmaɪz]	kundenspezifisch
information superhighway	[ˌɪnfə'meɪʃn 'suːpəˌhaɪweɪ]	Datenautobahn
teleworker	['telɪˌwɜːkə]	Bildschirmarbeiter/in
video-conferencing	['vɪdɪəʊ ˌkɒnfərənsɪŋ]	Videokonferenz
increasingly	[ɪn'kriːsɪŋlɪ]	zunehmend, steigend
graph	[grɑːf]	grafische Darstellung, Grafik
various	['veərɪəs]	verschiedene, mehrere

Ca

display *(v.)*	[dɪ'spleɪ]	zeigen, zur Schau stellen
annual	['ænjʊəl]	jährlich
major *(adj.)*	['meɪdʒə]	wichtig, bedeutend
sample	['sɑːmpl]	Muster, Probe
insight	['ɪnsaɪt]	Einblick
representative	[ˌreprɪ'zentətɪv]	Vertreter/in
socialize	['səʊʃəlaɪz]	sich unterhalten, gesellschaftlich verkehren
turnover	['tɜːnˌəʊvə]	Umsatz
involve	[ɪn'vɒlv]	*hier:* beinhalten, dazugehören

Cb

universal adaptor	[ˌjuːnɪ'vɜːsl‿ə'dæptə]	Universaladapter
catalogue	['kætəlɒg]	Katalog, Prospekt
portable	['pɔːtəbl]	tragbar

Da

security charge	[sɪ'kjʊərətɪ tʃɑːdʒ]	Sicherheitsgebühr
baggage claim check	['bægɪdʒ kleɪm tʃek]	Gepäckabholschein

Dc

duty-free	[ˌdjuːtɪ'friː]	zollfrei
board *(v.)*	[bɔːd]	an Bord gehen
departure lounge	[dɪ'pɑːtʃə laʊndʒ]	Abflughalle
label *(v.)*	['leɪbl]	beschriften, etikettieren

Dd

obligatory	[ə'blɪgətərɪ]	obligatorisch, bindend

De

compressed gas container	[kəm'prest gæs kən'teɪnə]	Druckgasbehälter
fireworks *(pl.)*	['faɪəwɜːks]	Feuerwerkskörper, Feuerwerk
explosive *(n.)*	[ɪk'spləʊsɪv]	Sprengstoff
unattended	[ˌʌnə'tendɪd]	unbeaufsichtigt
electronic device	[ˌɪlek'trɒnɪk dɪ'vaɪs]	Elektrogerät
interfere with s.th.	[ˌɪntə'fɪə wɪð 'sʌmθɪŋ]	etw. stören

Df

travel insurance	['trævl‿ɪn'ʃɔːrəns]	Reiseversicherung
loudspeaker	['laʊdspiːkə]	Lautsprecher

Unit 7

A

job advertisement	[dʒɒb əd'vɜːtɪsmənt]	Stellenanzeige, Stellenangebot
global	['gləʊbl]	weltweit, global
expansion	[ɪk'spænʃn]	Ausbreitung, Expansion
applicant	['æplɪkənt]	Bewerber/in
preferably *(adv.)*	['prefərəblɪ]	vorzugsweise
presentation	[ˌprezən'teɪʃn]	Präsentation, Vorstellung
keep s.o. informed	[kiːp 'sʌmwʌn‿ɪn'fɔːmd]	jdn. auf dem Laufenden halten
energetic	[ˌenə'dʒetɪk]	energisch
hard-working	[ˌhɑːd'wɜːkɪŋ]	fleißig
flexible	['fleksəbl]	flexibel
challenge *(n.)*	['tʃæləndʒ]	Herausforderung
résumé *(AE)*	['rezjuːmeɪ]	Lebenslauf
cover letter	['kʌvə 'letə]	Begleitschreiben
equal opportunities *(pl.)*	['iːkwəl‿ˌɒpə'tjuːnətɪz]	Chancengleichheit, Gleichberechtigung
division	[dɪ'vɪʒn]	Abteilung, Geschäftsbereich
manufacturer	[ˌmænjʊ'fæktʃərə]	Hersteller, Produzent
established in 1919	[ɪ'stæblɪʃt‿in‿'naɪntiːn‿ˌnaɪn'tiːn]	gegründet 1919
opening	['əʊpənɪŋ]	*hier:* freie Stelle
extensive	[ɪk'stensɪv]	umfassend, ausgedehnt
stable	['steɪbl]	stabil, fest
repeat business	[ri'piːt‿'bɪznɪs]	*hier:* Stammkundschaft

benefits *(pl.)*	['benɪfɪts]	Lohnnebenleistungen
relocation	[ˌriːləʊ'keɪʃn]	Standortverlegung
CV = curriculum vitae *(BE)*	[ˌsiː'viː] [kəˌrɪkjələm 'viːtaɪ]	Lebenslauf
recruiting manager	[rɪ'kruːtɪŋ‿'mænɪdʒə]	Leiter/in der Personalrekrutierung
experienced	[ɪk'spɪərɪənst]	erfahren
computer-literate	[kəm'pjuːtə 'lɪtərət]	über Computerkenntnisse verfügen
accounts receivable *(pl.)*	[ə'kaʊnts rɪ'siːvəbl]	Forderungen, Debitoren
accounts payable *(pl.)*	[ə'kaʊnts 'peɪəbl]	Verbindlichkeiten, Kreditoren
warranty	['wɒrəntɪ]	Garantie
benefit package	['benɪfɪt 'pækɪdʒ]	Sozialleistungspaket
medical	['medɪkl]	medizinisch
dental	['dentl]	*hier:* zahnärztlich
vacation *(AE)*	[və'keɪʃn]	Urlaub
working conditions	['wɜːkɪŋ‿kən'dɪʃnz]	Arbeitsbedingungen
people skills	['piːpl skɪlz]	die Fähigkeit, mit Menschen umzugehen; soziale Kompetenz
ambitious	[æm'bɪʃəs]	ehrgeizig
open-minded	[ˌəʊpn‿'maɪndɪd]	aufgeschlossen
desire *(n.)*	[dɪ'zaɪə]	Wunsch, Bestreben
travel agent	['trævl‿ˌeɪdʒənt]	Reisebürokauffrau/-mann
apply in writing	[ə'plaɪ‿ɪn 'raɪtɪŋ]	sich schriftlich bewerben
logistics	[lɒ'dʒɪstɪks]	Logistik
forwarding agent	['fɔːwədɪŋ‿ˌeɪdʒənt]	Spediteur, Spedition
operate a workstation	['ɒpəreɪt‿ə'wɜːkˌsteɪʃn]	eine Workstation/Datenstation bedienen
basic knowledge	['beɪsɪk‿'nɒlɪdʒ]	Grundkenntnisse
pressure	['preʃə]	Druck

Aa

appeal to s.o.	[ə'piːl tʊ 'sʌmwʌn]	jdm. gefallen, zusagen
requirement	[rɪ'kwaɪəmənt]	Anforderung

Ac

marital status	[ˌmærɪtl 'steɪtəs]	Familienstand
training course	['treɪnɪŋ‿kɔːs]	Aus-, Fortbildungskurs
educational background	[ˌedjʊ'keɪʃənl 'bækgraʊnd]	Bildungsweg
in chronological order	[ɪn‿ˌkrɒnə'lɒdʒɪkl‿'ɔːdə]	in chronologischer Reihenfolge
establish	[ɪ'stæblɪʃ]	*hier:* (Liste) festlegen, zusammenstellen
supervisor	['suːpəˌvaɪzə]	Leiter/in, Aufseher/in, Vorarbeiter/in
analyse	['ænəlaɪz]	analysieren
potential employer	[pə'tenʃl‿ɪm'plɔɪə]	mögliche/r Arbeitgeber/in
adapt to	[ə'dæpt‿tuː]	anpassen an
leadership capacities	['liːdəʃɪp kə'pæsɪtɪz]	Führungsqualitäten

demonstrate initiative	['demənstreɪt‿ɪ'nɪʃətɪv]	Initiative zeigen
organizational skills	[ˌɔːgənaɪ'zeɪʃənl skɪlz]	Organisationstalent
keep s.th. in mind	[kiːp 'sʌmθɪŋ‿ɪn maɪnd]	an etw. denken
job profile	[dʒɒb 'prəʊfaɪl]	Stellenbeschreibung
apprentice	[ə'prentɪs]	Auszubildende/r
professional experience	[prə'feʃənl‿ɪk'spɪərɪəns]	Berufserfahrung

Ba

assist	[ə'sɪst]	helfen, unterstützen
compute	[kəm'pjuːt]	rechnen, berechnen
coordinate	[kəʊ'ɔːdɪneɪt]	koordinieren, abstimmen
direct *(v.)*	[daɪ'rekt]	anweisen, anordnen
file *(v.)*	[faɪl]	(Akten) an-, ablegen, ordnen
launch *(v.)*	[lɔːntʃ]	(Produkt) auf den Markt bringen
process *(v.)*	['prəʊses]	ver-, bearbeiten
programme *(v.)*	['prəʊgræm]	programmieren
purchase *(v.)*	['pɜːtʃəs]	kaufen, erwerben
schedule *(v.)*	['ʃedjuːl]	(zeitlich) festlegen, planen
take inventory	[teɪk‿ɪn'ventərɪ]	Inventur/Bestandsaufnahme machen

Bb

sales campaign	[seɪlz kæm'peɪn]	Verkaufskampagne
expenses *(pl.)*	[ɪk'spensɪz]	Kosten, Spesen
sales strategy	[seɪlz‿'strætədʒɪ]	Verkaufsstrategie

Bd

deal with s.th. *(v.)*	[diːl wɪð 'sʌmθɪŋ]	sich mit etw. beschäftigen
foreign correspondence	['fɒrən ˌkɒrɪ'spɒndəns]	Fremdsprachenkorrespondenz
chair *(v.)*	[tʃeə]	den Vorsitz führen

Be

administrative assistant	[əd'mɪnɪstrətɪv‿ə'sɪstənt]	Verwaltungsangestellte/r
public relations assistant	[ˌpʌblɪk‿rɪ'leɪʃənz‿ə'sɪstənt]	Referent/in für Öffentlichkeitsarbeit
personnel manager	[ˌpɜːsə'nel 'mænɪdʒə]	Personalleiter/in

Ca

based on	[beɪst‿ɒn]	basierend auf, auf Grundlage von
exchange student	[ɪks'tʃeɪndʒ ˌstjuːdnt]	Austauschschüler/in
apprenticeship	[ə'prentɪʃɪp]	Ausbildung, Lehre
telemarketing	['telɪˌmɑːkɪtɪŋ]	Telefonvermarktung
individualized customer proposal	[ˌɪndɪ'vɪdʒʊəlaɪzd 'kʌstəmə prə'pəʊzl]	auf einen Kunden zugeschnittenes Angebot
interpret	[ɪn'tɜːprɪt]	interpretieren
statistical data	[stə'tɪstɪkl 'deɪtə]	statistische Daten/Angaben
related to	[rɪ'leɪtɪd‿tuː]	bezogen auf
present *(adj.)*	['prezənt]	gegenwärtig, aktuell

working knowledge	['wɜːkɪŋ‿'nɒlɪdʒ]	gute Grundkenntnisse
volunteer work	[vɒlən'tɪə‿wɜːk]	freiwillige Arbeit
tournament	['tɔːnəmənt]	Turnier, Wettbewerb
evaluate	[ɪ'væljʊeɪt]	bewerten
customer needs *(pl.)*	['kʌstəmə niːdz]	Kundenbedürfnisse
prospect *(v.)*	[prə'spekt]	(Kunden) (an)werben
native fluency	['neɪtɪv 'fluːənsɪ]	(beinahe) muttersprachliche Kompetenz

Cc

GCE "A" level (General Certificate of Education)	[ˌdʒiːˌsiː'iː‿'eɪˌlevl] ['dʒenərəl sə'tɪfɪkət‿əv‿ˌedʒʊ'keɪʃn]	Schulabschluss, vergleichbar dem deutschen Abitur
GCSE (General Certificate of Secondary Education)	[ˌdʒiːˌsiːˌes'iː] ['dʒenərəl sə'tɪfɪkət‿əv‿'sekəndrɪ‿ˌedʒʊ'keɪʃn]	Schulabschluss, vergleichbar der deutschen Mittleren Reife
Comprehensive school	[ˌkɒmprɪ'hensɪv skuːl]	Gesamtschule
Junior school	['dʒuːnjə skuːl]	Grundschule
Infant school	['ɪnfənt skuːl]	Grundschule (f.d. ersten beiden Jahrgänge)
Primary school	['praɪmərɪ skuːl]	Grundschule
Nursery school	['nɜːsərɪ skuːl]	Kindergarten
Pre Primary school	[ˌpriː'praɪmərɪ skuːl]	Kindergarten, Vorschule

Cd

compulsory education	[kəm'pʌlsərɪ‿ˌedʒʊ'keɪʃn]	Schulpflicht

Da

conclusion	[kən'kluːʒn]	*hier:* Schlusssatz
educational details	[ˌedʒʊ'keɪʃənl 'diːteɪlz]	Bildungs- und Ausbildungsweg
addressee	[ˌædre'siː]	Empfänger/in
introductory paragraph	[ˌɪntrə'dʌktərɪ 'pæragrɑːf]	einleitender Absatz, Einleitung
enclose	[ɪn'kləʊz]	beifügen
advertise	['ædvətaɪz]	inserieren, Reklame machen
sales territory	[seɪlz 'terɪtərɪ]	Verkaufsgebiet
recruit *(v.)*	[rɪ'kruːt]	(Mitarbeiter) einstellen, rekrutieren
salesforce	['seɪlzfɔːs]	Verkaufspersonal
implement	['ɪmplɪment]	aus-, durchführen, implementieren
field sales team	[fiːld seɪlz tiːm]	Außendienstteam
eager	['iːgə]	eifrig, begierig
call in	[kɔːl‿ɪn]	beraten
service *(v.)*	['sɜːvɪs]	bedienen, warten
merchandiser	['mɜːtʃəndaɪzə]	Verkaufsförderer
retail chain	['riːteɪl tʃeɪn]	Einzelhandelskette
achieve	[ə'tʃiːv]	zustande bringen

result-oriented	[rɪ'zʌlt‿ˌɔːrɪentɪd]	ergebnisorientiert
indicate	['ɪndɪkeɪt]	zeigen, anzeigen
qualification	[ˌkwɒlɪfɪ'keɪʃn]	Qualifikation, Befähigung
at your convenience	[ət‿jɔː kən'viːnjəns]	wenn es Ihnen passt
consideration	[kənˌsɪdə'reɪʃn]	Berücksichtigung, Erwägung

Dc

dictaphone	['dɪktəfəʊn]	Diktiergerät
capitalization	[ˌkæpɪtəlaɪ'zeɪʃn]	Großschreibung
punctuation	[ˌpʌŋktʃʊ'eɪʃn]	Zeichensetzung
graduate *(n.)*	['grædʒʊət]	Hochschulabsolvent/in
entry level	['entrɪ ˌlevl]	Einstiegsebene (Berufsanfänger/in)
grade average	[greɪd‿'ævrɪdʒ]	Notendurchschnitt
throughout	[θruː'aʊt]	durchweg
major in *(v.)*	['meɪdʒər‿ɪn]	als Hauptfach studieren
minor in *(v.)*	['maɪnər‿ɪn]	als Nebenfach studieren
economics *(pl.)*	[ˌiːkə'nɒmɪks]	Volkswirtschaft, Volkswirtschaftslehre
assignment	[ə'saɪnmənt]	Aufgabe
asset	['æset]	Aktivposten, Vermögen

Unit 8

Aa

send s.th. off	[send 'sʌmθɪŋ‿ɒf]	etw. abschicken

Ab

question s.o. *(v.)*	['kwestʃn 'sʌmwʌn]	jdn. befragen

Ac

select	[sə'lekt]	auswählen, aussuchen
pleased to do s.th.	[pliːsd‿tʊ duː 'sʌmθɪŋ]	etw. gerne tun

Ba

dress *(v.)*	[dres]	ankleiden, anziehen
elegant	['elɪgənt]	elegant, geschmackvoll
business suit	['bɪznɪs‿sjuːt]	Geschäftsanzug
sloppy	['slɒpɪ]	schlampig, nachlässig
casual	['kæʒʊəl]	lässig
sportive	['spɔːtɪv]	sportlich
smart	[smɑːt]	schick, flott
properly-dressed	[ˌprɒpəlɪ 'drest]	ordentlich gekleidet
self-confident	[ˌself'kɒnfɪdənt]	selbstbewusst
shy	[ʃaɪ]	schüchtern
insecure	[ˌɪnsɪ'kjʊə]	unsicher
reliable	[rɪ'laɪəbl]	zuverlässig
cheerful	['tʃɪəfʊl]	vergnügt
optimistic	[ˌɒptɪ'mɪstɪk]	optimistisch

relaxed	[rɪ'lækst]	entspannt
dynamic	[daɪ'næmɪk]	dynamisch

Bc

two-piece suit	[ˌtuː'piːs‿'sjuːt]	zweiteiliges Kostüm
silk	[sɪlk]	Seide

Bf

self-confidence	[ˌself'kɒnfɪdəns]	Selbstvertrauen
sincere	[sɪn'sɪə]	aufrichtig, ehrlich
handshake	['hændʃeɪk]	Händedruck
body language	['bɒdɪ 'læŋgwɪdʒ]	Körpersprache
resting	['restɪŋ]	ruhend
lap	[læp]	Schoß
nonverbal	[ˌnɒn'vɜːbl]	nonverbal
alert *(adj.)*	[ə'lɜːt]	aufmerksam, aufgeweckt

Bg

clarify	['klærɪfaɪ]	klären, klarstellen
academic *(adj.)*	[ˌækə'demɪk]	akademisch
performance	[pə'fɔːməns]	*hier:* Leistung
research *(n.)*	['riːsɜːtʃ]	*hier:* Nachforschungen
at this point	[ət‿ðɪs‿pɔɪnt]	zu diesem Zeitpunkt, jetzt
research *(v.)*	[rɪ'sɜːtʃ]	*hier:* nachforschen, sich informieren
assessment	[ə'sesmənt]	Einschätzung
strength	[streŋθ]	Stärke
weakness	['wiːknəs]	Schwäche
statement	['steɪtmənt]	Aussage
rely on	[rɪ'laɪ‿ɒn]	sich verlassen auf
career ladder	[kə'rɪə 'lædə]	Karriereleiter
goal	[gəʊl]	Ziel
candidate	['kændɪdət]	Kandidat/in
qualified	['kwɒlɪfaɪd]	qualifiziert
emphasize	['emfəsaɪz]	hervorheben, betonen
enthusiasm	[ɪn'θjuːzɪæzəm]	Begeisterung, Enthusiasmus
ahead of time	[ə'hed‿əv taɪm]	im Voraus
reflect	[rɪ'flekt]	widerspiegeln, reflektieren
clarity	['klærətɪ]	Klarheit
initial	[ɪ'nɪʃl]	anfänglich
delay *(v.)*	[dɪ'leɪ]	verzögern, aufschieben

Ca

extracurricular	[ˌekstrəkə'rɪkjələ]	außerhalb des Stundenplans

Cd

long- and short-term goals	[lɒŋ‿ənd ʃɔːt‿tɜːm gəʊlz]	lang- und kurzfristige Ziele

D

additional	[ə'dɪʃənəl]	zusätzlich

Alphabetical wordlist

Alphabetisches Wortregister

compulsory education **7Cd**
compute **7Ba**
computer rental **6Ac**
computer-literate **7A**
concerning **3A**
conclusion **7Da**
conference call **2Ee**
conference room **1D**
confirm **2Aa**
confirmation **3C**
consideration **7Da**
consulting *(n.)* **6Bf**
coordinate **7Ba**
corn **4Cc**
correspondence **3A**
corridor **1D**
courier **6Ac**
cover letter **7A**
cuckoo clock **4Da**
cucumber **4Cd**
currency exchange *(AE)* **6Ae**
customer needs *(pl.)* **7Ca**
customized **6Bf**
customs *(pl.)* **4Ac**
cutlet steak **4Cd**
CV = curriculum vitae *(BE)* **7A**

D

dash **2Dd**
data processing **1D**
date back **1Bb**
deal with s.th. *(v.)* **7Bd**
delay *(n.)* **3C**
delay *(v.)* **8Bg**
delayed **2De**
delivery date **3Ba**
demand *(n.)* **3Ae**
demonstrate initiative **7Ac**
dental **7A**
depart **5Ae**
department **1A**
departure **4Ac**
departure lounge **6Dc**
design *(v.)* **5Be**
desire *(n.)* **7A**
dessert **4Ca**
dictaphone **7Dc**
difference of opinion **6Ad**
direct *(v.)* **7Ba**
directions *(pl.)* **1Dc**
discount *(n.)* **3Ba**
discover **6Ba**
display *(v.)* **6Ca**
distribute **3Ab**
distributor **3Ab**
division **7A**
doll **4Da**
domestic flight **4Ac**
downtown *(AE)* **4Da**
dress *(v.)* **8Ba**
dry cleaning **6Ac**
duck **4Cd**
duty-free **6Dc**
dynamic **8Ba**

E

eager **7Da**
early-morning call **6Ae**
eastbound **4De**
economical **2Ee**
economics *(pl.)* **7Dc**
educational background **7Ac**
educational details **7Da**
effect *(v.)* **3Ba**
electronic device **6De**
elegant **8Ba**
elevator *(AE)* **1D**
emphasis **6Be**
emphasize **8Bg**
enclose **7Da**
enclosure **3Ab**
endlessly convenient **4Dd**
energetic **7A**
energy efficient **3Cd**
engaged *(BE)* **2Ab**
enquiry **3Ad**
enthusiasm **8Bg**
entry level **7Dc**
equal opportunities *(pl.)* **7A**
establish **7Ac**
established in 1919 **7A**
evaluate **7Ca**
event **6Bb**
exchange student **7Ca**
exclamation mark **2Dd**
exhibition **4Da**
exhibition hall **6B**
exhibitor **6Bf**
expansion **7A**
expenses *(pl.)* **7Bb**
experienced **7A**
expire **5De**
explosive *(n.)* **6De**
extension (number) **1Bf**
extensive **7A**
extract *(n.)* **4Da**
extracurricular **8Ca**

F

facilities *(pl.)* **5Bd**
fair *(n.)* **2Ca**
fairground **5Bd**
fare **4Dd**
favourable *(BE)*, favorable *(AE)* **3Ba**
feature *(n.)* **6Bf**
field sales team **7Da**
file *(v.)* **7Ba**
filing cabinet **1Ba**
finance department **1Ac**
fireworks *(pl.)* **6De**
fleamarket **4De**
flexible **7A**
flowchart **2Cd**
foreign correspondence **7Bd**
forwarding agent **7A**
freshen up **6Ba**
full stop *(BE)*/period *(AE)* **2Dd**
fully booked **5Bc**
fully-equipped **5Bd**

G

garlic **4Cc**
GCE "A" level (General Certificate of Education) **7Cc**
GCSE (General Certificate of Secondary Education) **7Cc**
Gents' **1D**
get around **4Da**

get back **1Ac**
get in touch **2Ca**
get on well **1Bb**
get settled in (job) **1Ac**
global **7A**
goal **8Bg**
goulash **4Ca**
grade average **7Dc**
graduate *(n.)* **7Dc**
grant a discount **3Ba**
grape **4Cd**
graph **6Bf**
guide *(n.)* **2Cd**

H

haddock **4Cd**
handshake **8Bf**
hard-working **7A**
have a seat **4Ba**
have s.th. at hand **2Aa**
head for *(v.)* **4Aa**
heated swimming pool **5Bd**
herb sauce **4Cc**
Here you are. **4Ba**
hesitate **1Ac**
high speed modem **3Ab**
hold s.o. liable for **3Ce**
Hold the line, please. **2Ba**
hole punch **1Ba**
hot beef tea **4Cb**
hourly **5Bd**
hyphen **2Dd**

I

I'd rather ... **4Ab**
imaginary **2Bg**
immediate delivery **3Cd**
implement **7Da**
in chronological order **7Ac**
in recent years **6Bf**
in view of **3Ab**
in-tray **1Ba**
increasingly **6Bf**
indicate **7Da**
individualized customer proposal **7Ca**
Infant school **7Cc**
information superhighway **6Bf**
initial **8Bg**
initial order **3Ab**
innovative **3Ae**
insecure **8Ba**
insight **6Ca**
interfere with s.th. **6De**
international code **2Ab**
interpret **7Ca**
interpreter **6Ac**
introductory paragraph **7Da**
introductory phrase **3Cb**
involve **6Ca**
issue *(v.)* **6Bf**
item **1Ba**
itemized **2Ee**

J

jet lag **5Af**
job advertisement **7A**
job profile **7Ac**
Junior school **7Cc**

K

keep s.o. informed **7A**
keep s.th. in mind **7Ac**
kidney pie **4Cd**

L

label *(v.)* **6Dc**
Ladies' (room) **1D**
lamb chop **4Cb**
lap **8Bf**
large-scale user **3Ab**
launch *(v.)* **7Ba**
laundry **6Ac**
leadership capacities **7Ac**
leaflet **3Bb**
leave a message **2Ba**
legally binding **3Cf**
lettuce **4Cd**
lightbulb **3Cd**
lobby **5Ba**
lobster **1Cc**
local call **2Ab**
location **5Be**
logistics **7A**
London-based **1A**
long- and short-term goals **8Cd**
long-distance call **2Ab**
look like **1Aa**
look s.th. up **2Ab**
loss **3Ce**
loudspeaker **6Df**
lounge **1D**
lunchtime **6Ba**

M

main course **4Cb**
major *(adj.)* **6Ca**
major in *(v.)* **7Dc**
make arrangements **2C**
manufacturer **7A**
map **4De**
marital status **7Ac**
market *(v.)* **4Ba**
market research **2Cc**
marketing assistant **1A**
marketing department **1A**
massage *(n.)* **6Ac**
match *(v.)* **1Ae**
medical **7A**
merchandiser **7Da**
mess **6Ba**
mineral water **4Cb**
minor in *(v.)* **7Dc**
miserable **4Cb**
mum *(inf. for mother)* **2Cc**
Munich **1A**
mushroom **4Cc**

N

native fluency **7Ca**
newsagent **4Dd**
next to each other **6Ab**
nonverbal **8Bf**
notice board **1Ba**
Nursery school **7Cc**

O

obligatory **6Dd**
obtain **3Cd**
occasionally **1Ce**
Oh dear! **6Ba**
on time **4Ac**

open-minded **7A**
opening **7A**
opening hours **2De**
operate **1Bb**
operate a workstation **7A**
operator **2Ee**
optimistic **8Ba**
optional **3Bb**
orange juice **4Cb**
order form **3Ca**
organization chart **1Ac**
organizational skills **7Ac**
out-tray **1Ba**
overnight **5Cd**

P

packing **3Ba**
parentheses *(pl.)* **2Dd**
parking lot *(AE)* **4Aa**
participate in **2Ca**
peach **4Cd**
people skills **7A**
performance **8Bg**
personnel department **1Ac**
personnel manager **7Be**
photocopier **1Ba**
pick up **2Ab**
pineapple **4Cd**
place an order **3Ca**
plaice **4Cb**
pleased to do s.th. **8Ac**
polite **2Aa**
pork fillet **4Cb**
portable **6Cb**
position **1Ab**
postcode *(BE)* **3A**
potential employer **7Ac**
potential supplier **3Ab**
poultry **4Cd**
powdered milk **1Bb**
prawn cocktail **4Cb**
Pre-Primary school **7Cc**
precisely *(adv.)* **2Aa**
preferably *(adv.)* **7A**
present *(adj.)* **7Ca**
present *(v.)* **3A**
presentation **7A**
press conference **6B**
press release **6Bf**
pressure **7A**
price reduction **4Dd**
Primary school **7Cc**
printed material **3Ba**
process *(v.)* **7Ba**
professional experience **7Ac**
programme *(v.)* **7Ba**
promise *(v.)* **2Ea**
promote **6Bf**
prompt **3Ca**
properly-dressed **8Ba**
prospect *(v.)* **7Ca**
public relations assistant **7Be**
punctuation **7Dc**
punctuation mark **2Dd**
purchase *(v.)* **7Ba**
put s.o. through **2Ba**

Q

qualification **7Da**
qualified **8Bg**
question s.o. *(v.)* **8Ab**
question mark **2Dd**
quotation **3Ab**
quotation marks, inverted commas **2Dd**
quote *(v.)* **3Ba**

R

rainbow trout **4Cb**
range **3Ab**
rapidly developing **3Ca**
reason *(n.)* **3Ab**
receipt **3Cd**
receive a phone call **2Aa**
receiver **2Ab**
reception desk **1Db**
receptionist **1D**
recruit **7Da**
recruiting manager **7A**
reduced price **6Ae**
reference **3Ab**, **3Cd**
reflect **8Bg**
refreshments *(pl.)* **4Ac**
related to **7Ca**
relax **6Ad**
relaxed **8Ba**
reliable **8Ba**
relocation **7A**
rely on **8Bg**
remain **3Bc**
remove **6Ae**
repeat business **7A**
representative **6Ca**
request *(n.)* **1Ca**
require **5Bc**
requirement **7Aa**
research *(n.)* **8Bg**
research *(v.)* **8Bg**
research and development department **1Ac**
research manager **1Ac**
reservation **5Ba**
response **1Ca**
rest *(n.)* **6Ba**
restauration works **4Da**
resting **8Bf**
result-oriented **7Da**
résumé *(AE)* **7A**
retail chain **7Da**
return address **3Ab**
return flight **5Ad**
ring up **5Bc**
roast turkey **4Cc**
room service **5Bd**
round brackets **2Dd**
routine **6Ba**

S

salad garnish **4Cc**
sales agreement **3Ba**
sales campaign **7Bb**
sales department **1Ac**
sales manager **1Ac**
sales strategy **7Bb**
sales territory **7Da**
salesforce **7Da**
salutation **3Ab**
sample **6Ca**
sauna **5Bd**
sauté **4Cc**
scampi **4Cc**
schedule *(v.)* **7Ba**
seafood **4Cd**
secretarial service **5Bd**